5/21/98

Dear Mom and Dad,

We're sorry that you didn't get to go to Isreal for the Fiftieth Anniversary, but we know that this book will be just as good. And, it will help you plan for your next trip there, if you manage not to move again for a little while.

Love,

Greg and Alyson

Micha Bar-Am

ISRAEL
A PHOTOBIOGRAPHY

Micha Bar-Am

The First Fifty Years

ISRAEL

A PHOTOBIOGRAPHY

Essay by

Thomas L. Friedman

THIS BOOK WAS MADE POSSIBLE
BY A GENEROUS DONATION FROM
THE SCHUSSHEIM FOUNDATION, HAIFA.

PRODUCTION OF THE BOOK WAS SUPPORTED
BY THE GENEROSITY OF
HANNO D. MOTT, NEW YORK.

SIMON & SCHUSTER EDITIONS
Rockefeller Center
1230 Avenue of the Americas
New York, New York 10020

Photo editor: **Orna Bar-Am**
Designer and graphic editor: **Joseph Jibri,** Tel Aviv
Translator/editor of Bar-Am texts: **Marsha Pomerantz**

Manufactured in Italy by A. Mondadori Editore
10 9 8 7 6 5 4 3 2 1

Library of Congress Cataloging in Publication Data
Bar-Am, Micha
Israel, a photobiography: the first fifty years/
Micha Bar-Am; essay by Thomas L. Friedman
p.   cm.
1. Israel—History—Pictorial works. I. Friedman, Thomas L.
II. Title.
DS126.5.B25   1998   97-36404
956.9405'022'2—dc21   CIP

ISBN 0-684-84513-X

Pages 2–3, *Sinai, 1980.*
Pages 4–5, *Trekking in the Negev, 1950s.*

CONTENTS

***O**n the road to Jerusalem, War of Independence, 1948.*
Photo by Robert Capa.

Notes

Micha Bar-Am

***D**avid Ben-Gurion proclaims independence, Tel Aviv Museum, May 1948.*
Photo by Robert Capa.

Shortly before noon on May 14, 1948, the British left Haifa Port. In a brief, spare ceremony, the commander of British forces saluted the Union Jack and, to the accompaniment of bagpipes, the flag was lowered and folded. The commander stepped into a motor launch that took him from the dock to the battleship awaiting him in the harbor. It was the end of thirty years of British administration in Palestine.

I watched this historic scene as a seventeen-year-old, standing with dozens of British officers and a few civilian port workers like myself on the roof of the port authority building abutting the dock. A few hours later, at 4:00 on a Sabbath eve, David Ben-Gurion was to announce the establishment of a Jewish state and to read its declaration of independence. Fearing last-minute intervention from the British, the provisional People's Council had chosen a "secret" place to convene, the Tel Aviv Museum. Rumor of the imminent event spread, of course, and hundreds of people were gathered outside the museum on posh Rothschild Boulevard, anxiously awaiting developments: how a nation is born.

At midnight of the very same day, the armies of five Arab nations—Syria, Egypt, Transjordan, Lebanon, and Iraq—invaded the new Jewish state with the declared intention of "wiping out the Zionist entity within ten days." The next day I left Haifa, the port from which I'd dreamed of sailing off into the big world, and headed inland to join friends already fighting in the Jerusalem hills.

Twelve years earlier, at the age of five, I had docked in Haifa with my family. It was shortly after the beginning of what the Arabs called "the Arab revolt," the British called "the disturbances," and the Jews called "the riots." The uprising, a widespread protest against Jewish immigration, included strikes and attacks against the Jews and the British.

My father, the son of refugees from Russia, had become a well-to-do businessman in Germany. But sensing the political tremors of the thirties, he had sold his share in the thriving family business and brought his wife, son, and two daughters to Palestine, where he planned to begin life anew as a pioneer and farmer. He had at his disposal only the money he had salvaged from the old country and an inexplicable optimism. He ended up putting both into what seemed like a suitable investment for a land with a blazing Mediterranean climate: an ice factory. Before long the ice factory, which happened to be in the Arab quarter of downtown Haifa, went up in flames. The family fortune melted and, with it, my romantic dreams of exploring far-off lands. My father's optimism survived. Lacking both Hebrew and a trade, he found work as an unskilled laborer, in road construction.

By then World War II was well under way. I was ten and went to a Hebrew elementary school, where I also studied classical Arabic—reading and writing—as well as French and English. I picked up a little spoken Arabic on frequent strolls through the markets.

I had a special relationship with the Arabic teacher, Mr. Shmueli, a Jew from Iraq. He was a kindly man tormented by many of my classmates who, given the prevailing atmosphere, couldn't stand the subject. During school vacations he used to visit the Bedouin tribes around Beersheba, and my parents agreed to let me go with him. We spent long evenings in Bedouin tents listening to legends and parables, the narration punctuated by rounds of dark, bitter coffee whose taste and aroma, mingled with the thick smoke of the campfire, remain with me to this day.

Between one parable and the next, Mr. Shmueli managed to combine a little business with pleasure, trading in sheep to supplement his modest salary. From my corner of the tent I used to watch him in the heat of negotiation, his body language adding impact to his verbal claims. Amid the endless murmur of speech and the rhythmic grinding of coffee beans I fell asleep.

*I*mmigrants pose with portraits of Theodor Herzl, founder of modern Zionism, Mishmar Hashiv'a, 1949.
Photo by Robert Capa.

I started photographing at an early age. I don't know what impelled me most: curiosity, the magic of the picture, the hunter's pride at bagging a bit of reality, the prospect of adventure.

Always forgetful, I adopted the camera as a memory aid, a means of gathering information, organizing thoughts, holding on to images. Then it didn't matter if "the real thing" slipped away.

During the War of Independence there was no time to ponder what was most real: we were living it, preoccupied with survival. I didn't have a camera of my own, and took no photos.

At the end of the war I was released from active duty and with a group of friends—all of us nineteen or twenty years old—went north to set up a new kibbutz on the Lebanese border. We cleared rocks from the fields and began to plant. While most of my friends concerned themselves with crops and livestock, my restless nature pulled me elsewhere: I did guard duty on horseback, taking the opportunity to slip off from time to time to visit Bedouin encampments along the border and Arab and Druze villages throughout the Galilee. An avid amateur archaeologist, I attached myself to digs in the Judean Desert in the search for what came to be known as the Dead Sea Scrolls. I borrowed cameras from friends on the kibbutz.

My life changed when I finally bought my first Leica—vintage 1930, the year I was born. In a small notebook I began recording the exposure times and lighting conditions of every photo I took and, gradually, by trial and error, I taught myself photography. On weekends I would display my work on the bulletin board in the communal dining hall, and eventually my photos began to be published.

I've been working in photography for nearly fifty years now, mostly in Israel and often on assignment. The initiative for a story may be mine or an editor's, but it is usually prompted by events in the news or at the center of public debate.

Within this professional framework, which offers me a challenge, a platform, and a pretext for being involved, I can range widely, with relative freedom. I keep my internal eye open for that other, metaphorical image that transcends illustration to achieve a wholeness of its own. I strive for the elusive entity that is both evidence and evocation, public record and personal vision.

Working at the scene of the action, I have adopted Robert Capa's saying: "If your photographs aren't good enough, you're not close enough." But in retrospect I add a corollary: If you're too close to events, you lose perspective. It is not easy to be fair with the facts and keep your own convictions out of the picture. It is almost impossible to be both a participant in events and their observer, witness, interpreter. The effort brings great reward, and equally great frustration.

The roles of observer and participant came into contrast during two exchanges I had on the second day of the Yom Kippur War. When, in the midst of the shock and confusion, I arrived at a forward position in Sinai, laden with cameras and other equipment, a young soldier barely out of basic training glanced at me and said, "Listen, I can see why you're here, a war photographer and all, but I'm only eighteen. Can you tell me what the hell *I'm* doing here?"

Later the same day, when I was walking among the troops and looking for a unit I could "adopt," someone called to me: a tall, slim, smiling man, an officer in an elite commando unit, whom I finally recognized as the son of a good friend from the kibbutz. He told his friends how he used to sit on my knee. Then he looked at me, puzzled, and said, "Listen, I'm here because I have to fight, but you, with your cameras, what are *you* doing here?"

Sometimes the distinction between observer and participant fades. Later I accompanied that unit, which was given orders to break through enemy lines to a besieged outpost known as "Budapest," on the Suez Canal near the Mediterranean Sea. I was there to document particular moments—which would be the last for some of us, maybe myself—in a particular place: calm blue sea, clean wet sand, saline marshes radiating white heat, soldiers marching as shells fell around us, Sager missiles whistling over our heads and slamming into the tanks that gave us cover, soldiers picked off by the Egyptian snipers who outnumbered us. With nightfall, a decision was made to withdraw. My camera was irrelevant as all of us still standing helped support the injured and carry the wounded and dead.

Occasionally the observer/participant dichotomy brings with it more irony than grief. Two weeks into the war, Israeli forces were outside the city of Suez and Egyptian lines were crumbling. My colleague Shlomo Arad and I, unarmed, accompanied a tank unit, riding in a requisitioned pickup truck with a recalcitrant driver. We decided to leave both on the main road and continue on foot toward an apparently abandoned missile site, hoping to find both photogenic subjects and alternative transportation.

On the way, attempting to comfort myself with a familiar voice and ward off the evil eye, I called into the desolate silence in Arabic: "Come out with your hands up!" The only other sound was the rumble of distant artillery. Taking photos of the missiles, we spotted just what we were looking for:

*I*mmigrant transit camp, Tiberias, 1950.
Photo by Robert Capa.

a jeep that seemed intact. We were on our way to take possession when suddenly, out of trenches, one at a time, eighteen dusty, startled Egyptian soldiers emerged with their hands in the air.

No less stunned than they, we watched them toss their weapons in a pile, and recovered enough presence of mind to order them to tie one another's hands. We got into the jeep and marched them ahead of us to the main road, gave them cigarettes and a jerrican of water, and directed them toward an assembly point for POWs.

We had captured eighteen prisoners with our cameras, we realized later, but not a single image of the encounter.

My whole life, personal and professional, has been intertwined with Israel's history. Over the years I have photographed current events inside my house, at my front door, in the backyard. My archive is stuffed with fragments of reality: thousands of images arranged in drawers and boxes. Sifting through it to create a book of predetermined format and limited scope has required the judgment of hindsight. I make no claim that the resulting picture is balanced, objective, or complete. Though the characters and events are real, the contexts in which I have placed them are my responsibility alone.

*O*ld City walls, Jerusalem, 1967.

Israel at Fifty

By Thomas L. Friedman

**Tomb of the Patriarchs,
Hebron, 1997.**

When I moved back to America in the late 1980s, after serving as *The New York Times*'s Jerusalem correspondent, I brought home a snapshot to hang on my office wall to remind me of my time in Israel. I was intrigued to see that my old friend and former *New York Times* Israel photographer, Micha Bar-Am, chose an almost identical image for his collection of photographs of Israel at fifty.

My picture shows a tall tree on the grassy banks of the Sea of Galilee. The sea stretches out in the background as smooth as a blue blanket. It is a picture of serenity. But as you look a little closer you notice something slightly odd. At the foot of the tree, where flowers should be blooming or two lovers nestling, there is a steel barrel dug into the ground. All you see is the top of this steel barrel, and painted on its lid are two Hebrew words: Security Hole. This barrel is a steel garbage can that police use to deposit suspicious packages or actual bombs that have been discovered. These security holes are found all over Israel, like fire hydrants. They accidentally find their way into the background of family vacation photographs, school field-trip snapshots, or postcard panoramas.

Even tourist scenes. One of Micha's shots shows the ancient Islamic structure that contains the Tomb of the Patriarchs, a site holy to both Jews and Moslems and that dates back 5,000 years. The picture would indeed make a great postcard, except that looming in the foreground is a sign. In any other country it might say Please Don't Litter, or Have a Nice Day. In Israel it says: Security Pit.

I dwell on these pictures because they capture an essential truth about Israel. What makes the country so fascinating to write about and to photograph, what gives it its almost fatal attraction at times, is that it is full of tensions and contradictions between war and peace, hope and despair, the modern and the ancient, the East and the West, the religious and the sacrilegious, the Arab and the Jew, the Jew and the Christian. I always like to say that everything in Israel is about itself and something else. A sidewalk is a sidewalk, and a road where Jesus walked. A wall is a wall, and the place where Joshua fought the battle of Jericho. A hole is a hole, and a bomb disposal device. A hill is a hill, and a biblical landmark. Even the number fifty isn't just fifty—it's also the biblical Jubilee year, when all slaves were freed, all mortgaged lands were restored to their original owners, and all fields were left untilled.

Consider the picture Micha has included of four watermelons stacked by the side of a road (page 57). On the top melon someone has etched the Star of David—symbol of the state of Israel. This is what catches your eye in the photograph. And you immediately wonder, why the Jewish star on a watermelon? Who knows why? Maybe someone just had nothing to do with his pocket knife, or maybe the farmer who grew the watermelons was trying to signal potential buyers that these melons came from a Jewish farmer, not an Arab one. Or maybe it was a historical reference, for this etched star evokes the yellow stars Jews had to wear under the Nazis. Such is the politics of fruit in Israel. When you live in a country with so much history, where every square inch has been claimed and reclaimed by one tribe or nation, nothing ever seems innocent or accidental. Nothing is ever just itself. There is always the thing and the something else.

These layers and tensions also explain why, as it turns fifty, Israel engenders two very contradictory reactions. Some days Israel feels like such a young fifty-year-old, and some days Israel feels like such an old fifty-year-old. Some days it seems so new, alive, fresh, open, and capable of any kind of innovation—the ultimate postindustrial state. And some days it feels so encrusted, so scarred, so war-weary, like a country that was born and then immediately became an adult, with no chance for a carefree adolescence. Some days you wake up in Jerusalem and you are sure that the future has buried the past, and other days you wake up terrified that the past has just buried the future.

To contemplate Israel at fifty is to contemplate the titanic struggle going on every day there between the forces that make it old and the forces that keep it young. To write about Israel at fifty is to write about this struggle. To photograph Israel at fifty is to depict this struggle in color and black and white.

*J*erusalem, 1985.

The struggle that fascinates me most about Israel is the one related to those security holes peppered around the country. The first thing you have to learn as a reporter or photographer covering Israel is this: Israel is not just a conflict, it's a country. That may seem utterly obvious, but it's not to a lot of people. So many people outside of Israel know about it, think about it, read about it, watch it on television, or debate about it in school as though it were just a conflict. To be sure, Israel has been in conflict all its life. The founding generation, with the ambivalent support of the international community, established a Jewish state in its ancient homeland—against the wishes of Israel's Arab neighbors and Palestinian inhabitants. And Israel has really never known a full day's peace with all its neighbors.

If Israel were just about this conflict, though, things would be simple. But the fact is that Israelis refuse to be defined by the conflict. The fact is that they insist on being able to play, malinger, invent, flirt, make love, vacation, work, picnic, and die of old age—despite the ongoing conflict—and this produces the most interesting tension in Israel, between the ever-present battlefront and daily life. Even though the battlefront is so close, and sometimes right out the front door, there is a constant struggle to keep the two separate.

You can see this struggle running through many of Micha's photographs of Israel. There is the man barbecuing in a park (page 129). You see him adjusting the meat on the coals while his children turn somersaults in the grass. The man is at ease. He's wearing only an undershirt for a top. But after you have taken in this bucolic scene, your gaze drifts to the bottom left of the picture and you notice that the man has a pistol tucked into his pants. On the previous page you find a father sitting in his front yard, bouncing his young son on his lap, while another of his children sits naked, splashing in a baby pool. It's your average family on a weekend, except that the barefoot father is wearing a camouflage army uniform. One of my favorites is Micha's picture of a fashion show at a women's army base (page 97). Micha stood on one side of the fashion runway and, focusing through the legs of a model, took a picture of a bleacher full of Israeli women soldiers watching this style parade on their own parade ground during a break from training. The fashion runway meets the military runway. That's the real Israel. It's not a country defined by women soldiers. And it's not a country defined by fashion shows. It's a country defined by women soldiers attending fashion shows even as they learn how to operate radar that will track incoming missiles from Iraq.

Micha and his wife, Orna, had a fight over whether to include one particular picture in this book, showing the birth of a baby boy (page 127). The boy's name is Barak. He was born on the eve of the 1967 war, and he is Orna and Micha's son. Micha was reluctant to include the photograph (which he took), but Orna wanted it in, because for her it spoke volumes about another abiding tension that runs through Israeli life. It is the tension between a society that loves children, indulges them, dotes on them, is virtually organized around them, and then, at age eighteen, turns them all into soldiers and sends them off to military duty.

This tension is particularly acute, as Orna notes, for the mother of sons. Because from the moment that baby is delivered and the nurse says the Hebrew word *ben*, meaning "boy," every Israeli mother starts to worry. She starts to count the days until her son will join the army. It's a mental calendar ... ten years to go ... five years to go ... one year to go. ... And then once he's in the army she counts the months and watches the map. Will he be assigned to Lebanon? Nablus? Hebron? Or, G-d willing, a desk job? Every mother secretly wishes for a desk job, every son openly aspires to join an elite unit—ideally the air force, but failing that, the naval commandos, or maybe the chief of staff's antiterrorist team. It is no wonder that Israel is the only country where people's moods soar and dive on the basis of what they hear hour by hour on the radio news. The beep-beep-beep that comes at the top of each hour announcing the news reminds me of one of those heart monitors, only it's hooked up to the country's heart, giving an hourly status report on its vital signs. And it all goes back to that moment of birth, and the clock that starts ticking when the nurse announces *ben* or *bat*, boy or girl. To listen to the radio news in Israel is not simply an information-gathering exercise. It's a way of tracking your kids and the dangers they might face at any moment. It has an urgency to it, which every Israeli parent understands.

This celebration of children, and the silent countdown that every Israeli parent engages in before that child puts on a uniform and takes up a weapon, also, paradoxically, explains the longevity of the peace process. Part of Israel's never-ending quest to remain a country, not just a conflict, involves learning how to deal with constant security threats without becoming so hardened that the society becomes something ugly. You see this vividly in the debates over whether and how much Israeli security services should be allowed to use torture to interrogate suspected terrorists in order to prevent acts of violence that have been planned but not yet executed. You also saw it during the Palestinian uprising, or Intifada, in the late 1980s, when Israeli soldiers found themselves in endless confrontations with rock-throwing Palestinians. The Israelis had a clear superiority in arms. That is, they had the guns and the tanks while the Palestinians had stones and flaming bottles. But both sides felt that they had the same thing at stake: communal survival. So the issue came down to this question: Was Israel justified in using live ammunition against Palestinians armed only with stones, even though both sides were fighting for the same thing, communal survival, and Israelis were certain that if Palestinians had had access to more lethal force they would have used it?

Dining room, *Kibbutz Kinneret, 1979.*

The prominent Israeli political theorist Yaron Ezrahi has argued that Israelis tried to resolve this debate by introducing the rubber bullet during the Palestinian uprising. The bullet says, "We are at war, even if we share the same sidewalks." But the rubber coating says, "I don't want to kill you outright if I don't have to, because we are neighbors and we will have to share the same sidewalks." The bullet says, "I will not tolerate what you are doing to me, because I know you really want my house." And the rubber coating says, "I can't tolerate what this occupation of your house is doing to me. We will win, but at a terrible price to our own moral fabric." That price can be summed up by one of Micha's pictures widely reproduced in the 1980s (page 82). It shows a group of Palestinians, hoods over their heads with little holes to see through, sitting in the back of an Israeli vehicle. They are informers enlisted by the Israeli army to point out those who are guilty at a roundup of Palestinian suspects. They wear the hoods so they will not be identified as they inform on their neighbors. There is something about the process of selecting who is guilty and who is not, who will go to prison and who will go free, that evokes some very bad memories for every Jew. Yet, this is a bad neighborhood. There is no doubt that among those being informed on are people really plotting or committing violence against Israelis. That's why there is tension.

While the rubber bullet is how Israelis try to cope with this tension, the peace process is how they try to resolve it. Think about it for a second. The peace process is a constant triumph of hope over experience. I don't know how many times I have heard officials declare or pundits chime or average people wail after some particularly ghastly terrorist incident: "That's it. The peace process is over." And then, lo and behold, a few days later, the sun is out again, the glass is swept up, the bodies are buried, the wounded begin healing, and someone floats a new idea to get the parties together, and the peace process is born anew.

Why does it keep coming back? Because that quest for normalcy, that desire to be only a country and not a conflict, runs so deep in Israelis that they will chase almost any rainbow if they think that at the end of it they will discover a place where there is no battlefront, no reserve duty, no security holes—only normal life. This is the secret that always keeps the peace process afloat. It's not that Israelis believe that Yasir Arafat has had therapy and has become a lover of Zion. It's not that they trust him. It's that at some level most Israelis understand that they will never be able to relax, never be able to take that gun out of their waistband, if there is no settlement.

And the reason the right-wing nationalist arguments have never triumphed in Israeli diplomacy, even when the right wing is in power, is that ultimately Israelis will never fully accept the determinism of the right. That determinism says the Arabs will never willingly tolerate a Jewish state in their midst, they can never be trusted, no lasting peace with them is possible, and therefore Israelis must either fight here heroically or die here humiliated. Those arguments may one day be proven correct, but the reason that Israelis keep trying to prove them wrong is that to accept those arguments is to accept that all there is to look forward to is a future full of yesterdays. That insight drove Yitzhak Rabin to take great risks for peace. Rabin was never sure there was an Arab-Palestinian partner for a secure peace with Israel, but he was sure that as the leader of Israel he owed it to himself, to this generation and to future generations, to keep testing. That testing cost him his life, but even his death could not stop the inexorable march of the peace process he did so much to advance. Too many Israelis refuse to live with a future full of sandbags, if they can at all avoid it. Where you can really feel the depth of that sentiment is among the large number of bereaved parents who have lost family members to war or brutal acts of terrorism but who nevertheless remain ardent advocates of the peace process. What they all say is that the pain they have experienced from the loss has not left them hungry for revenge but rather with an ache in their hearts that is so great, so infinite, they never want it experienced by anyone else.

And that's why you can take the peace process and tear it, bend it, staple it, crumple it, rip it, fold it, singe it, soak it in gasoline, and set it ablaze, but there's one thing you can't do and that's stop it. It's like the biblical burning bush: It may look like it's on fire, but it's never consumed.

Micha captures that resilience in one particular picture in this book—a family portrait (page 181). His wife and two sons, wearing gas masks, are huddled together in a room. The image was taken during the Gulf War as Israel was being hit with Iraqi Scud missiles, and the Bar-Ams were doing what every Israeli family did at the time—taking shelter in a tape-sealed room of their house. There is a slightly extraterrestrial quality to this family photo of mother and sons in gas masks. But what gives it its special character is that right in the middle of the scene, in Orna's lap, is the family cat—sans gas mask, of course—looking as normal as ever. Something about the cat staring out from the laps of these gas-masked human beings is life-affirming. It is the one normal living creature in an altogether scary and abnormal photograph. That cat is the living reminder of a normal life that existed before the sealed room and can exist after it. The peace process is that cat, only it has even more than nine lives. Many, many more.

One of the nicest aspects of working in Israel as a writer or photographer is the sheer intimacy of the place. I don't know of any other country where you can find so many great stories on one tank of gas. I remember one week Micha and I drove down to the southern tip of Israel to do a story about Kibbutz Yotvata, where they have cows that produce the best milk in Israel. Something about the dry desert air those cows like. Everywhere we went—from the kibbutz, to Eilat, to Taba—we kept bumping into friends of Micha's, all of them characters of one sort or another, including Israel's original beach bum, Rafi Nelson. One week later, Micha and I had to take a drive up to Metulla at the northern tip of Israel, on the border with Lebanon. As we drove into Metulla, we needed to ask directions, and we came upon a man who was standing at a crosswalk. I rolled down my window to get his attention and as this gentleman took a look inside our car he shouted, "Micha, how are you!" I accused Micha of staging the whole encounter. One week it's his pals in Eilat, the next week it's in Metulla. As the famous Israeli song about the elite Palmach army unit in the 1948 War of Independence goes: "From Metulla to the Negev, from the sea to the Judean desert, every young man to arms, all the nation is on guard." And Micha seemed to know them all, north, south, east, and west. Indeed, he has a saying that always used to make me chuckle. "Israel is divided in two: There is the half that I know and the half that knows me."

That was once true for many Israelis. It isn't quite the case any longer, which brings up another tension that runs through Israeli life today. It is the tension between the intimate Israel that so many Israelis grew up in—where everyone seemed to know everyone else (and everyone else's business)—and the Israel of today, which is simply a much bigger, much more impersonal, more materialistic, more competitive, less egalitarian society, where the demands of the individual increasingly take precedence over those of the community. The little neighborhood shopkeepers are slowly being replaced by the huge shopping malls of Jerusalem and Tel Aviv. There are more high-tech compa-

nies from Israel on the New York Stock Exchange today—more than seventy—than from any other foreign country other than Canada. With a per capita income of nearly $16,000 in 1997, Israel's standard of living outstrips that of Spain and Greece and is about equal to that of Great Britain. In a space of twenty years Israel has gone from being a country most famous for exporting oranges to one that will probably soon be importing fruit because so many fields have been turned over to high-tech factories.

When you arrive at Ben-Gurion Airport and drive through the gate into Israel, one of the first things you see today is a huge billboard-size cellular phone displaying the time and date. It is illuminated at night, like some postmodern menorah. (Just down the road, though,

***O**utside the Old City, Jerusalem, 1969.*

after you pass the giant cell phone, there is an equally giant photograph of the late great Lubavitcher rebbe, Rabbi Menachem Schneerson. That's Israel!) Israeli paratroopers march off to the Lebanon front armed with an Uzi in one hand and a cellular telephone in the other to call home. It wasn't long before Israeli soldiers stationed in Lebanon got into trouble for ordering pizzas from northern Israeli border towns and having them delivered at the border fence. An Israeli friend said his sister became worried one day after she realized that her son, a paratrooper stationed in Lebanon, must be on a mission deep inside that country. How did she know? Her son hadn't telephoned from Lebanon for two days, which meant to her that he must be outside the range of his cell phone.

As Israel has grown bigger and more prosperous (make no mistake, though, there are still plenty of urban and rural poor there), the balance between the state and the individual has shifted. As Israeli political theorist Ezrahi points out, Israel has gone from being a country "defined by history to a country increasingly defined by autobiography—from a country animated by the epic Jewish narratives of exile and return, and held together by a communal struggle for national liberation, to a prosperous, pluralistic country, where individual gratification is now glorified, and where the monumental story of the redemption and ingathering of a people is increasingly challenged by a symphony of individual voices." In this transition, something is gained and something is lost. What is gained is greater space for individual creativity, for satisfying one's own needs, even for personal indulgences. But what is lost is a degree of frontier intimacy and simplicity that gave Israeli life a unique quality, especially compared with other modern Western societies in the late twentieth century. It may not be fair, but it is hard not to wince when you are driving along some ancient biblical route and run into the golden arches of McDonald's.

Indeed, if Israel in its first fifty years was preoccupied with turning the desert green and attracting immigration, its next fifty years is likely to be preoccupied with how to keep even a sliver of that green so that the millions of Jews who flocked to the Promised Land will want to remain living there. For the first time, there is real tension between Israel's longing for immigration and the environmental strains this is putting on such a tiny country. Forget about Peace Now. If the war with the Arabs is ever settled, the next big new party in Israel will be called "Green Now." In 1997, the *Ha'aretz* newspaper quoted a study by the Israeli urban planner and architect Adam Mazor that found that Israel is already among the most crowded nations in the West. Mazor was heading a government committee, Master Plan 2020, which was charged with drawing up plans for Israel in its pending "Age of Crowding." By 2020, according to Mazor, Israel will house up to 8 million people (it currently holds around 5 million) and its population density will reach 857 persons per square kilometer, compared with 400 persons in Holland and 26 persons per square kilometer in the United States. *Ha'aretz* said, "Preposterous ideas such as creating artificial islands in the Mediterranean are on the drawing board.... Just recently, plans were submitted (but not approved) for a 70-story building in downtown Jerusalem."

The communal intimacy that once characterized Israeli life and that the country is struggling to preserve is captured in a picture of four mothers talking on the sidewalk in a kibbutz (page 108). At first glance, the picture seems unremarkable. But when you look at it closely you realize that it is full of action: Everyone in the picture is connected. One mother has her right hand on her own baby's carriage and her left hand on that of a neighbor to whom she is speaking. Her neighbor is holding her baby in one arm, and while she is talking to the first woman, her baby is reaching out to the third woman, who is kissing the baby's hand while holding her own carriage with her left hand. Then, just out of the picture frame, a fourth mother is sitting on a bench. All you see is her hand on the third mother's carriage. It is a human chain, a microcosm of Israel as family. Four mothers, three strollers, one country.

Zionism, the founding ideology behind the establishment of the modern Jewish state, was a revolt against the ghetto existence that had, for so many years, characterized Jewish life in Eastern Europe and Russia. But while Zionism was a revolt against the ghetto, the early Zionists never wanted a clean break. They wanted to draw on the Jewish values, traditions, and bonds of solidarity forged in the ghetto, but they wanted to be unchained from them as well. In that sense, Zionism was both a synthesis and a constant tension between new and old ideas. It drew on one of the oldest themes in Judaism, the longing to return to Jerusalem after centuries of exile, and fused it with the newest theme of Judaism, leaving the ghetto and re-entering history by building a Jewish state with its own modern Jewish citizenry. The Nazis' genocide against the European Jews added an urgency to Zionism, making the return of Jews to their ancient homeland and their creation of a modern state not simply an ideological fascination but a necessity for survival.

When Israel was born in 1948 you could say that the tribe with the oldest past suddenly had the youngest future. And ever since then there has been a struggle to determine the balance between the bonds of identity that link Israel with its past and the demands of development that will power Israel into the future. Israel still has not found the perfect balance and probably never will. The tension is always there, however, as Israelis try to remember the past and forget the past, to remain loyal to the aspirations of both their grandparents and their grandchildren.

That tension remains strongest and most incendiary in the area of religious practice. One of the most revolutionary aspects of modern Israel was that it declared to all Jews that after years of being defined by their wandering and homelessness they would now be a people with a home, where all who identified themselves as Jews could take their shoes off and settle. The founding fathers of Israel believed that Israel should have no official brand of Judaism. They wanted any man or woman who was born Jewish or converted to Judaism to feel at home there, whether they were secular, Orthodox, ultra-Orthodox, Reform, Conservative, or Reconstructionist; left-wing or right-wing; Ashkenazi or Sephardi. The idea of the founders was that Israel would somehow mediate all those different strands and tensions and keep them living together in a single family, albeit an occasionally tense one.

But the founders of Israel and the leaders of the Labor Party, who dominated Israeli political life from 1948 to 1977, were themselves devoutly secular people. Many of them were attracted to

Zionism as a rebellion against the religious life and mentality of their grandparents. They left religion exclusively to the Orthodox rabbis and parties, who reminded them of their grandparents. And for the first three decades of the state, the Orthodox parties dutifully joined every Labor government and confined their interests and demands largely to ensuring that their religious institutions were properly funded and that Orthodox rabbis and traditions dominated religious affairs in Israel, from births to burials. All of this started to change in 1977, when the right-of-center Likud first ousted the Labor Party from power. Suddenly, Israel was now evenly split between two major blocs, with the religious parties able to tip the balance between them. This gave them real political power, which they started to wield outside the traditional areas of religious affairs.

Their desire to do so was reinforced both by their growing numbers and by their own sense of living under siege. Many Orthodox in Israel are sincerely frightened by the forces of globalization. They fear that as the walls fall between Israel and her Arab neighbors, as Israel becomes tightly integrated into the global economy, and as McDonald's, Blockbuster Video, and 500 cable stations all come marching in, Israel's Jewish character will be lost or diluted. They do not want a future in which their grandchildren and Yasir Arafat's grandchildren will all make microchips together. They really do fondly remember the cultural, religious, and communal intimacy of the European ghettos. They also believe, with some justification, that without their devotion to tradition and Jewish religious practices, much of Judaism could be lost in another generation or two.

***F**estival of Hebrew Song, Arad, 1997.*

Arrayed against them are those Israelis who have little use for religious tradition. They want to be part of the powerful economic and social currents in the world today, and they see the peace process as a bridge to globalization. These secular Israelis believe that living in a Jewish state, where Jewish holidays are national holidays, where the Sabbath is an official day of rest, and where an essential part of their children's education is Jewish history and culture, is enough Judaism.

By Israel's fiftieth birthday, secular and religious Israelis complain of being besieged by each other. This sharpening struggle is something every Jew should be concerned about. After all, Israel is the embodiment of the shared destiny of the Jewish people and if it cuts itself off from large blocks of Reform, Conservative, and secular Jews around the world, this would have a devastating effect. Think of it this way: For centuries Jewish life was held together in the Diaspora by Torah, by traditional observance, and by the ghetto walls. When the ghetto started to crumble in the nineteenth century and Jews were free to enter the world, a strict interpretation of Torah could no longer hold them together. Reform and Conservative Judaism arose as a response to this situation. Fortunately, though, just as the ghetto walls were collapsing, the Zionist movement also emerged. Zionism, and ultimately the Jewish state, became the new focus and carrier of Jewish identity for many Jews. Israel declares that Jews will continue Jewish history not just through Torah and observance but through this living reality of a Jewish state. That's why the struggle for Israel's soul is so important. The Israeli state must always remain a framework within which the different streams of Judaism—Orthodox, Reform, Conservative—can debate with each other. Israel should mediate that debate, but it should not decide its outcome. The prime minister of Israel is not a theologian. If, under pressure of domestic politics, an Israeli government were forced to anoint Orthodox Judaism as the only official, legitimate religion, it would fracture the unity of the Jewish people worldwide. The danger of the country's fracturing from within is a very real one. This is my biggest concern as Israel turns fifty.

Most analysts assumed this would be the case: that as the threat from outside diminished, the internal divisions within Israel—divisions that were limited or muted because of the need to pull together in the face of an external enemy—would erupt with full force. Every country faces such internal strains and Israel is no exception. But in the wake of Prime Minister Yitzhak Rabin's assassination, in light of the ups and downs in the Oslo peace process, and given the deepening tensions among Orthodox, Conservative, Reform, and secular Jews in Israel, one has to worry whether Israel will end up with the worst of all worlds: a smoldering war within and a smoldering war without.

In this regard, I am particularly drawn to Micha's photograph of a world Jewry conference in Jerusalem (page 178), which Yitzhak Shamir, the Likud Party leader in the late 1980s, was attending along with Shimon Peres, the Labor Party leader of the day. At the close of the conference Mr. Shamir has turned and is shaking hands with someone to his right and Shimon Peres has turned and is shaking hands with someone on his left. Shamir and Peres have their backs to each other, and they are both standing directly under a seal of the state of Israel and a banner that reads: "Conference on Jewish Solidarity."

I have never been very objective when it comes to writing about Israel, because I, like so many others who have been touched by this Jewish state, care too deeply about its fate to stand back and remain aloof. Like so many Jews, I feel that my own identity is in some way bound up in who wins this battle in Israel between the forces that would make it old, closed, and pessimistic, and those that would keep it open, optimistic, and young. And this sense of connection applies to many non-Jews as well. There is something about the Holy Land that touches us all. Somehow if peace can reign there, somehow if the oldest of tribes can learn to live together, a hope for peace is stirred everywhere. And when turmoil reigns there, when it seems as though the cradle of civilization is splintering, a pall is cast far beyond Israel's borders. Even as a modern state, Israel is about itself and something else.

For me, this story of Israel at fifty can be reduced to two photographs in this book, both of women. One shows a blond Israeli woman soldier, who is teaching a young boy to read Hebrew at an immigration absorption center in Kfar Saba (page 29). There is something utterly fresh about this blond Israeli soldier-woman. She shines like a newly minted coin. And the way she is absorbed in teaching this young boy makes them look, quite literally, like two links in the chain of generations that binds Israel to its past and its future. But most of all in this picture of soldier and child there is optimism—the hope that Israel will be not just a conflict but a country, not just a country but a mission, not just a mission but a home. Everything that keeps Israel young is in that photograph.

The photograph I contrast with it is one that Micha took of the late Israeli prime minister Golda Meir while she was riding in a helicopter with her top military brass (page 131). Golda has her head cradled in her hand and her hair is a blend of gray and black: the color of worry. She is dressed in a dowdy gray outfit. In the background is Army Chief of Staff Haim Bar-Lev and in the front is a pilot who seems to be telling them that he's about to take off. But Golda is indifferent to everything around her. Her gaze is to the floor. Her visage is the essence of the tired, agonized Jewish mother. For 5,000 years Jewish mothers have struck that pose, only this Jewish mother is the prime minister. Somehow everything that makes Israel old, everything that etches lines in its face, everything that turns a prime minister's hair gray—from wars to internal divisions to pressures of absorption—is captured in that photograph.

Both these pictures deserve the same caption: "Israel at Fifty."

Have no doubt, though, about which one I'm rooting for. Indeed, on this fiftieth anniversary of Israel's founding, when I think of my wish for this country, it would be found in the last verse of that old Bob Dylan song "Forever Young":

"May your hands always be busy/ May your feet always be swift/ May you have a strong foundation when the winds of changes shift/ May your heart always be joyful/ May your song always be sung/ And may you stay, always, forever young."

THE PHOTOGRAPHS

*O*n the road to Sde Boker, 1950s.

THE EARLY YEARS

Modern Zionism is the fulfillment of the longing Jews have felt for Zion (Jerusalem) and the biblical land of Israel since their first expulsion, by the Babylonians, 2,600 years ago. Spurred by both the awak

ening of nationalism in nineteenth-century Europe and an increase in anti-Semitism there, a small stream of immigrants made its way to Palestine, and Jewish settlement grew steadily.

After the collapse of the Ottoman Empire in 1918, Palestine was designated a British Mandate by the League of Nations. Britain had stated in the Balfour Declaration of 1917 that it

Haifa Port, 1950s.

viewed "with favor . . . the establishment in Palestine of a national home for the Jewish people," adding that it wished to do nothing that would "prejudice the civil and religious rights of existing non-Jewish communities in Palestine." The result was a restriction of Jewish immigration.

Even after World War II the British refused to grant free entry to the survivors of concentration camps and to other Jews displaced by the war. Immediately after the state of Israel was established in 1948, masses of immigrants arrived, first from Europe, then from the Middle East and North Africa.

On the eve of the 1948 War of Independence there were about 600,000 Jews in Palestine and about twice as many Arabs. During the next ten years the Jewish community doubled its numbers. The "ingathering of exiles" from vastly different social, cultural, and economic backgrounds created tensions that persist to this day.

Immigrant from Romania, Haifa Port, 1950s.

pages:

Independence Day parade, Haifa, 1950s. A crowd scans the sky for the air force flyover
that will be part of a military parade. The public display of might was reassuring to a young

Kiryat Gat immigrant transit camp, 1950s. Immigrants eked out a living with whatever skills they could offer. Because of the shortage of permanent housing, some lived for years in the clusters of tents or shanties set up to provide temporary accommodation for the flood of arrivals.

Mermelstein Pharmacy, Afula, 1957. Waiting for a prescription to be filled, an Arab woman from a nearby village nurses her infant and keeps a firm grip on her means of transportation. Afula, not far from Nazareth, was founded in 1925 by immigrants from the United States and is now the largest town in the Jezreel Valley.

***A** teacher-soldier in the Kfar Saba transit camp, 1958.* A nineteen-year-old kibbutznik tutors a boy recently arrived from North Africa. In the 1950s many women did their regular army service as teachers and social workers and were vital in integrating immigrants.

***B**anana harvesters, Kibbutz Gesher Haziv, 1956.* Whatever work they had done in their former lives, these immigrants from Romania, with limited Hebrew, resorted to seasonal agricultural work in Israel. They were hired labor rather than members of the kibbutz.

Sabras, **Kibbutz Degania Bet, 1954.** Radiating innocence and optimism, three native Israelis symbolize the hope of a new nation in which Jews would have more control of their destiny. All three eventually became officers in the army. One (*left*) went into business management, a second (*center*) became an industrial engineer. The one on the right was killed in the Six-Day War and buried beside his father, who had died defending Degania in 1948.

House call, Azata transit camp, 1958. A doctor working as a volunteer makes his rounds among immigrants in the Negev Desert. A gynecologist by training, he also served as a pilot in the air force reserves.

T*orah study, Moshav Porat, 1960.* The parents of these boys immigrated from Libya in 1950 and set up a moshav, or semicollective farming community. Most of the immigrants from North Africa were traditional and supplemented their children's general education with religious studies.

Army reservists, Western Galilee, 1955. The prolonged state of no-war-no-peace between Israel and its neighbors has resulted in a defense strategy based on a small regular army and extensive reserves that are called up in emergencies. Most men are subject to about a month's reserve duty each year up to the age of fifty-five. Army service has helped integrate segments of society that otherwise might not come in contact with one another. It has also fostered what some call a boys'-club atmosphere among Israeli men, and what others call male bonding.

Kibbutz Gesher Haziv, 1956. Standing in the doorway of the chicken coop, members of this Western Galilee kibbutz founded in 1949 take a morning break for conversation. Kibbutzim, with their joint ownership of property and their principles of equality and self-sufficiency, are Israel's unique contribution to ideological settlement. Over the years they have evolved, developing industry, accommodating themselves to the country's increasing capitalism, and allowing more privacy and private property.

F*irefight, northern border, 1957.* A border guard armored vehicle evacuates farm workers from disputed territory in the upper Galilee after Syrian soldiers opened fire from positions on the Golan Heights. Skirmishes like this one made control of the Heights a matter of contention.

Egyptian prisoners, Sinai Campaign, 1956.

THE SINAI CAMPAIGN

To demonstrate his growing independence of the West, in 1956 Egyptian President Gamal Abdel Nasser nationalized the Suez Canal, previously an international waterway. Israel made common cause with France and Britain, which each had an interest in the canal, and launched the Sinai Campaign in October.

Israel had its own reasons for the campaign. The canal and the Tiran Straits, at the southern tip of Sinai, had been closed for years to ships flying the Israeli flag or carrying goods to Israel. The resulting sense of siege had been intensified by deadly cross-border raids from Egyptian-controlled Sinai.

Within the campaign's first hundred hours, the Israeli army captured the Gaza Strip and Sinai and stopped, by prior agreement with its allies, about twelve miles from the canal. Britain and France occupied part of the canal zone. The United States and the Soviet Union, both fearing a loss of influence in the area, pressured all three countries to withdraw, as did the United Nations.

Israel, completely isolated, pulled back early in 1957. The government's decision to give in to international pressure and relinquish control of Sinai set off a bitter debate throughout the country. Israel did regain passage through the Tiran Straits, though access to the Suez Canal was not restored until the peace agreement with Egypt twenty-two years later.

Demonstration against the withdrawal from Sinai, Jerusalem, 1957. Ben-Yehuda Street was a frequent venue for demonstrations because it was close to the Knesset, which has since moved to new quarters across town. Today Ben-Yehuda Street is a pedestrian mall, complete with cafés and street performers.

Border guard, Jerusalem hills, 1960. A border guard unit is briefed for a nighttime ambush of infiltrators coming across from Jordan.

Previous pages:

Defense wall, Jerusalem, 1960. The War of Independence had left Jerusalem divided, with the western part under Israeli control and the eastern, including the Old City, in the hands of the Jordanians. Makeshift walls were put up to block sniper fire from the Jordanian side. The concrete cones at left are "dragon's teeth," which can be lined up to block tanks. The nuns, from the Romanian Orthodox monastery in West Jerusalem, were on their way to prayers in the Old City.

Old City walls, Jerusalem, viewed from the west, 1966. On the laundry line are the fringed garments worn by Orthodox Jewish men as reminders of the 613 commandments.

DAVID BEN-GURION

Born in Poland in 1886, Ben Gurion came to
Palestine in 1906 and first reached prominence as
one of the leaders of the Jewish labor movement.
With the establishment of the state, he served simulta-
neously as Israel's first prime minister and its defense
minister. After a political dispute in 1953, he resigned
and settled at Kibbutz Sde Boker, in the Negev. His
great vision had been the development of the desert,
and though he later returned to government, he spent
his last years at the kibbutz, where he died in 1973.

David Ben-Gurion, Kibbutz Sde Boker, 1966.

***D**avid Ben-Gurion, Ramat Poriya, 1960.* When Syrian artillery on the Golan Heights shelled Israeli farming settlements in the Jordan Valley, Israel attacked the Syrian positions. Ben-Gurion, again prime minister and defense minister, met with soldiers after their foray.

David Ben-Gurion, Kibbutz Sde Boker, 1966. Ben-Gurion took his morning constitutional in the company of bodyguards and advisers, talking to them whenever he moved his trademark transistor radio away from his ear. On the eve of his eightieth birthday, his bodyguards agreed to back off and allow a photo that captured the man and the expanse.

REMEMBERING

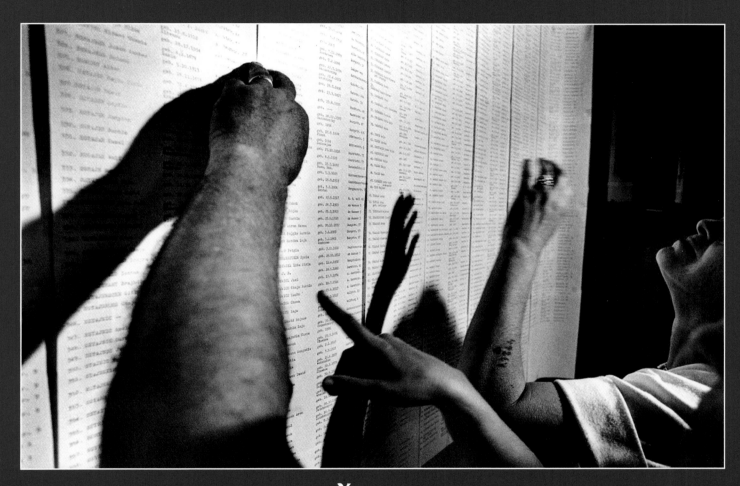

Yad Vashem Holocaust memorial, Jerusalem. The search for missing relatives continues to this day. "Hand and Name" is the literal meaning of Yad Vashem, and *yad* also means "memorial." Yad Vashem contains an archive and exhibition center dedicated to the memory of Jews killed by the Nazis.

Eichmann trial, Jerusalem, 1961. For years Israel's intelligence agency, the Mossad, tracked Nazis who had escaped to Argentina and lived there under false identities. Finally, in 1960, it kidnapped Adolf Eichmann, who had headed the Gestapo's Jewish affairs department, and brought him to Israel to be tried for his role in the genocide of European Jews. The trial riveted Israelis and attracted tremendous interest internationally. What was newsworthy was not only the shocking detail from living witnesses but Israel's role in seeking justice on behalf of the Jewish people.

After a reading of the fifteen charges against him, from the extermination of Jews, Poles, Gypsies, and others, to the theft of property, Eichmann stood up and said that he had been only a cog in the Nazi machine: "In the sense of the charges, I am not guilty."

The court found Eichmann guilty on all counts. He was sentenced to death and hanged, the only case in the history of Israel in which the death sentence has been carried out. The trial had a profound influence on Israeli attitudes toward the Holocaust. The "new Jew," raised to be tough, had found the vulnerability of European Jews difficult to grasp and embarrassing to acknowledge. But after the trial, more survivors began to talk about their experiences, and more native Israelis were able to listen.

Housing project, Tel Aviv, 1970s.

THE SIX-DAY WAR

In the spring of 1967 tension was high on the borders with both Egypt and Syria, which were allies and rivals for leadership in the Arab world. Egyptian President Nasser, whipping up Cairo mobs into a war frenzy, threatened Israel with annihilation, but this time the situation went beyond rhetoric. Nasser demanded the withdrawal of the UN forces that had been a buffer in Sinai since 1956, and again closed the Tiran Straits. Israelis, under siege, sensed that their sliver of land could easily be overrun by neighbors who vowed to throw them into the sea.

Israel finally launched a preemptive strike on June 5, wiping out Egypt's air force on the ground. Syria and Jordan joined the war the same day, Jordan with an artillery barrage on West Jerusalem. In the next six days Israeli forces captured the Sinai Peninsula from Egypt, the Golan Heights from Syria, and East Jerusalem and the West Bank from Jordan.

Soldier at the Western Wall, Jerusalem, June 1967. The remnant of the Temple in Jerusalem had been under Jordanian control since the 1948 war, and Jews had been denied access. This paratrooper, one of the first to reach the Wall in the midst of the war, was notable for his utter calm and the way the bullets draped over his shoulders seemed to transform themselves into a prayer shawl.

The Temple—originally built by King Solomon, destroyed by the Babylonians, rebuilt, and later destroyed by the Romans—was long the principal site of worship for Jews. Until the establishment of Israel, the Western Wall was called the Wailing Wall, a focus of longing in the Diaspora.

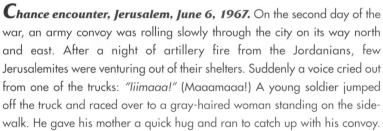

Chance encounter, Jerusalem, June 6, 1967. On the second day of the war, an army convoy was rolling slowly through the city on its way north and east. After a night of artillery fire from the Jordanians, few Jerusalemites were venturing out of their shelters. Suddenly a voice cried out from one of the trucks: *"Iiimaaa!"* (Maaamaaa!) A young soldier jumped off the truck and raced over to a gray-haired woman standing on the sidewalk. He gave his mother a quick hug and ran to catch up with his convoy.

Paratroopers, Old City, Jerusalem, June 1967. King Hussein's decision to join the war prompted Israel to divert to Jerusalem the paratroopers who were about to go to Sinai. The battles with Jordan's British-trained Arab Legion were fierce and casualties on both sides were heavy.

***B**attle by night, Jerusalem, June 1967.*

***T**he Kidron Valley (Valley of Jehoshaphat), Jerusalem, June 1967.* A makeshift flag flutters from an army vehicle moving past tombs that date from the Second Temple (515 B.C. – A.D. 70). Both Jewish and Muslim traditions regard this valley, below the Mount of Olives, as a likely site for resurrection on the Day of Judgment.

Temple Mount, Old City, Jerusalem, June 1967. The sheikh in charge of the mosques on the Haram a-Sharif (known to Jews as the Temple Mount) watches Israeli soldiers at the Western Wall, which they had captured just a few hours earlier. The Haram, from which Mohammed is said to have ascended to heaven, is the third holiest site for Islam, after Mecca and Medina. The Wall forms a side of its base.

Whatever the sheikh was thinking, it had probably been thought before on this site, which had been changing hands for 3,000 years. The Romans, after destroying the Jewish Second Temple, built a temple to Jupiter here; the Byzantine Christians used the site as a garbage dump. With the Arab conquest in the seventh century A.D., two mosques were built: al-Aksa and the Dome of the Rock. The Crusaders turned the Dome of the Rock into a church after their conquest in 1099; Muslim Sultan Salah a-Din (Saladin), taking control almost ninety years later, restored the mosques.

Dome of the Rock, Old City, Jerusalem, June 1967. Israeli paratroopers captured the Old City and took control of the Temple Mount on the third day of the war. In the foreground are flags they seized from the Jordanian army.

Under Defense Minister Moshe Dayan, an agreement was reached after the war on control of the holy sites. The Muslim religious authority, the Waqf, continued to oversee the Temple Mount (Haram a-Sharif), and Jewish religious authorities were in charge of the Western Wall.

B*ereaved father, Golan Heights, 1967.* In a ceremony at a former Syrian army base, parents accept battle decorations awarded posthumously to their sons.

Refugees, Silwan, 1967. Facing Israelis on an armored vehicle, the refugees
are framed by the helmet of one soldier and the machine gun of the other.

***R**efugees, Allenby Bridge, West Bank, 1967.* The bombed-out bridge over the Jordan River was replaced by a temporary structure and reopened to traffic after the war. Named by the British after General Edmond Allenby, commander of the forces that captured Palestine from the Turks in World War I, the bridge remains the principal crossing point between the West Bank and Jordan.

MOSHE DAYAN

Dayan, born on Kibbutz Degania in 1915, was a charismatic commander and influential in shaping Israel's army. Defense minister during the Six-Day War, he sought to initiate dialogue with Palestinians in the West Bank and the Gaza Strip as soon as the fighting ended. This photograph was taken in a refugee camp in the West Bank as part of a cover shoot for *Life* magazine. Asked by *Life* photographer Cornell Capa if he wasn't afraid to go there unarmed and without bodyguards so soon after the war, Dayan shrugged. "Either I'll get a cup of coffee," he said, "or I'll get a bullet. There's no in-between." At a small roadside café in Kalandia, on the way to Ramallah, Dayan was immediately recognized and offered a stool. He sat down, coffee arrived, and the conversation—in fluent Arabic—began.

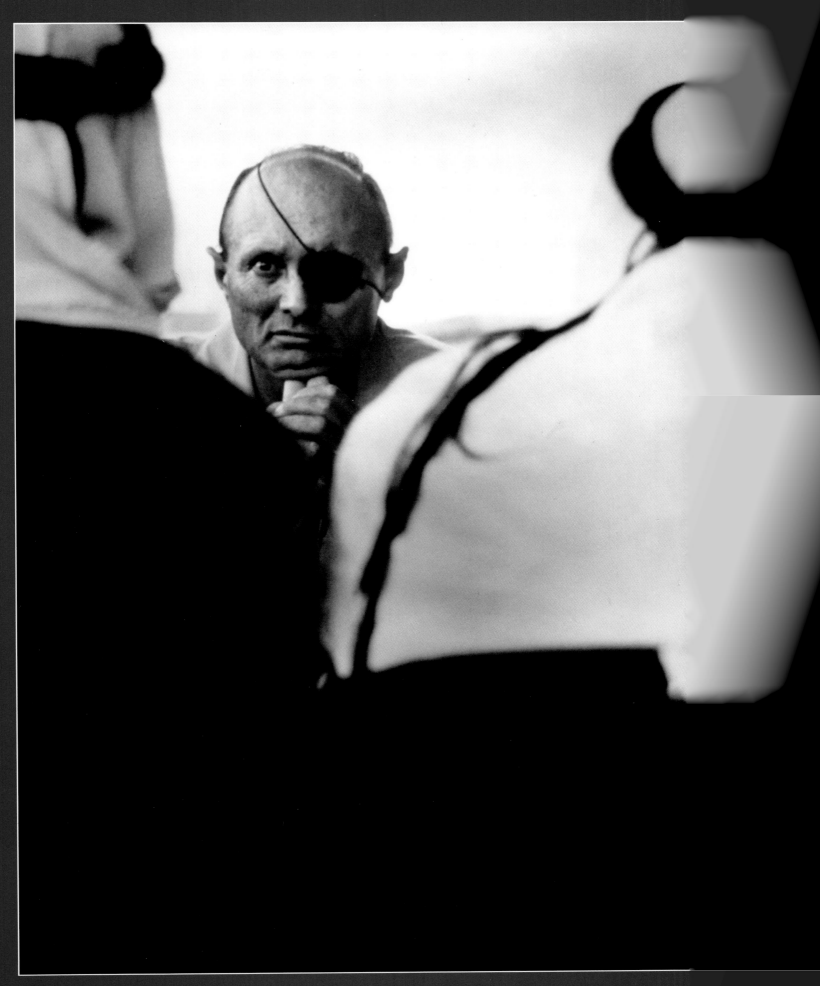

Moshe Dayan, Kalandia refugee camp, West Bank, 1967.

Kafr a-Labed, West Bank, 1967. After an attack on a border kibbutz, Israeli forces combed the area for clues. When they found tracks leading across the border to Kafr a-Labed, they gathered all the men in the village center and demanded that they turn over the perpetrators.

***B**riefing, Judean Desert, 1971.* Soldiers conclude maneuvers with a review of the maps. The backdrop, an abandoned house, had now become a target for firing practice.

Return from a night patrol, Jordan Valley, 1968. When infiltration from Jordan increased between 1968 and 1973, the army intensified its border patrols along the Jordan River. The valley became known as "Land of the Manhunt."

***P**risoners of war, Golan Heights, 1970.* Exchanges of fire with Syria on the Golan Heights escalated into a series of battles called the "Three-Day War."

***P**alestinian informers, West Bank, 1967.* These collaborators with Israel wear sacks over their heads as disguises. Sitting in a car with police or intelligence officers, they review a lineup of villagers paraded past them and point out those suspected of hostile activity.

Lineup of suspects, West Bank, 1967.

Palestinian informers, West Bank, 1967. The Hebrew sticker on the windshield is a security warning to soldiers, like the World War II slogan "Loose lips sink ships." Literally: "The price of chatter is blood."

D*eir al-Balah refugee camp, Gaza Strip, 1969.* A Palestinian woman carrying a load of sticks for firewood stops and stares as soldiers conduct a house-to-house search.

The Gaza Strip, on the Mediterranean coast north of Sinai, has been a crossroads for traders and conquerors since ancient times. Refugees from the 1948 war more than doubled its population, and a high birth rate and debilitating poverty have made it politically explosive.

*P*risoners of war, Golan Heights, 1970.

Funeral, Kibbutz Massada, Jordan Valley, 1968. Three members of this kibbutz near the Jordanian and Syrian borders were killed when their tractor hit a mine on the kibbutz banana plantation. Hundreds of people from neighboring kibbutzim joined the mourners.

Checkpoint Erez, 1970. Before dawn each day laborers from the Gaza Strip line up at this major point of entry into Israel; they will be picked up by contractors on the other side. Despite the stringent security checks and the low pay, the lack of alternatives in Gaza makes this grueling routine a necessity. Israel's economy,

in turn, has become dependent on Palestinian labor. But in recent years, as terrorist attacks or intelligence warnings result in lengthy border closures, Israel has begun to fill the vacuum with temporary workers from Romania, Nigeria, Colombia, the Philippines, and other countries not involved in the conflict.

Roundup, Gaza Strip, 1969. After an attack on Israeli troops, soldiers searching for suspects close off the area and check IDs. Israel clamped down severely on Gaza Strip Palestinians after an increase in attacks, carried out mainly by residents of the refugee camps.

DAILY BREAD

Father Neophitus, Santa Katarina Monastery, Sinai, 1967. It was 3:00 or 4:00 A.M. The Greek Orthodox priest had just finished baking bread and was back in his cell for a glass of ouzo and a hand-rolled cigarette. In the morning the bread would be given to Bedouin in the area in accordance with an agreement made centuries ago, which guaranteed the safety of the small group of monks among tribes that were initially hostile.

Santa Katarina, a fortress as well as a monastery, was established by the Byzantine emperor Justinian in the sixth century, at the foot of what is believed to be Mount Sinai, where Moses received the Ten Commandments. With the rise of Islam in the seventh century, the monks appeased the Muslims by building a mosque within the monastery compound. The monastery has notable collections of icons and Greek and Arabic manuscripts.

Immigrants, Neve Sharett, 1968. Soviet Jews, long denied exit visas, began to arrive in Israel in the late 1960s in a wave of immigration that continued for several years. Thanks to Israel's improved economy, the housing the government supplied was a far cry from the shanties of the 1950s.

***W**omen soldiers in basic training, Tzrifin army base, 1970.* The mother of one of the soldiers observes a parade marking the end of basic training. Most Israelis begin army service as soon as they finish high school, men serving for three years and women for just under two. The transition from sheltered home life to the demands of army routine is not easy for conscripts or for their parents, who tend to become addicted to the hourly radio news.

Fashion show, Tzrifin army base, 1973. With a fashion runway laid down on the parade ground, hundreds of women soldiers get a glimpse of what they might be wearing if they were not in khaki.

Among the roles that women fill in the army is training male soldiers in combat units—artillery, tanks, missiles—without themselves engaging in combat.

Parade, Beersheba, 1973. Beersheba, called the capital of the Negev, has grown from a small administrative center for Bedouin tribes in the south to a city of about 150,000 residents—an industrial, commercial, and cultural center with a major hospital, a university (Ben-Gurion University of the Negev), a music conservatory, and a Hilton hotel.

Via Dolorosa, Old City, Jerusalem, 1968. In the rare years when their calendras coincide, Good Friday pilgrims walk the Via Dolorosa just when Jews are making their way to Passover prayers at the Western Wall. Since Friday is the Muslim holy day, Muslims heeding the muezzin's call complete the mix.

A parting of the ways, 1967.

Preparing for Yom Kippur, Mea Shearim, Jerusalem, 1967. At 5:00 A.M. on the day before the Day of Atonement, this man is taking a live chicken home for the custom of *kaparot*, in which he will symbolically transfer his sins to the bird and swing it in a circle above his head to disperse them. The principle is that of the ancient scapegoat custom, in which the high priest of the Temple would transfer the community's sins to a goat and send it off into the desert. The chicken, however, will be slaughtered and eaten.

Easter, Old City, Jerusalem, 1989.

Talpiot, Jerusalem, 1968. An old sentry post has turned into a notice board. The post, of the kind the British called a "pillbox," is on the Bethlehem Road, close to the pre–Six-Day-War border with Jordan.

***T**aba beach, Sinai, 1982.* Near the border between Israel and Egypt, sisterhood bridges the culture gap between sunbathers and Bedouin.

***G**reek pilgrims, Old City, Jerusalem, 1972.* Easter is celebrated on different dates by the Western, Russian Orthodox, and Greek Orthodox churches, drawing pilgrims and tourists each time.

***K**ibbutz Givat Haim (Ihud), 1973.* Kibbutzim developed out of a blend of late-nineteenth-century European romanticism, socialism, and Zionism. For immigrants from Poland and Russia in the early part of this century, the ancient Jewish homeland seemed the perfect place for a new society based on equality and a return to nature. As they cleared boulder-strewn land and malarial swamps for agriculture, fierce ideology and the pragmatism of shared means allowed them to survive. Despite the equality of opportunity on which the kibbutzim were based, however, women have tended to take on traditional roles.

On the train to Jerusalem, 1970. When the Temple was the focus of religious observance, it was customary to bring sacrificial offerings to Jerusalem three times a year on the holidays that coincided with harvest times: Passover, Shavuot, and Sukkot. The tradition of pilgrimage continues, with variations on the theme.

Tel Aviv Zoo, 1974.

*F*lag-seller, Jaffa Road, Jerusalem, 1977.

Farmer, Metulla, 1966. This resident of Metulla, on the Lebanese border, supplemented his farm income by driving the village's only taxi. He chose to pose in his spare kitchen.

P*rotest demonstration, Mea Shearim, Jerusalem, 1967.* Ultra-Orthodox Jews—a category that in fact includes many different communities—are non-Zionist or anti-Zionist. Though they identify with the biblical land of Israel, many believe there should not be a Jewish state until the Messiah comes. They do, however, participate in Israeli politics to pursue their own goals. Because Israel's multiparty system usually means that their support is required to form a coalition government, they wield more political power than their numbers in the population would suggest (under 5 percent, a quarter of those who identify themselves as observant).

Subjects that touch off protests among the ultra-Orthodox include driving near religious neighborhoods on the Sabbath, autopsies, archaeological digs that may disturb ancient Jewish graves, and recognition of the Reform and Conservative movements in Judaism.

Hebron, 1976. Rabbi Moshe Levinger, among the first of the Jewish settlers in the West Bank town of Hebron after the Six-Day War, addresses a rally protesting the alleged desecration of Jewish books by Arabs.

The incident that sparked the rally took place in the nearby Tomb of the Patriarchs, holy to both Muslims and Jews because their common ancestor, Abraham, bought the site, the cave of Machpela, as a family burial ground. Jews and Arabs lived peaceably in Hebron for many years, but the slaughter of more than sixty Jews by their neighbors during Arab rioting in 1929 ended Jewish settlement there. Levinger and others point to the massacre as a reason for Jews to demonstrate their resolve and renew the community in Hebron.

Land Day, Taibe, 1980. When the government expropriated Arab-owned land in the north of Israel in 1976, protests ensued and six people were killed. Arab citizens of Israel earmarked the day, March 30, for annual rallies in the pursuit of their rights.

الذكرى الرابعة ليوم الأرض المجيد

D*emonstration, Tel Aviv, 1971.* Hospital employees in administration and maintenance, among the lowest paid in Israel, demand improvements in salary and work conditions.

Rabbi Meir Kahane, Jerusalem, 1984. A native of the United States and the founder of the Kach movement, Kahane went to Israel in 1971 and tried to import his politics of xenophobia, calling for the expulsion of West Bank and Gaza Strip Palestinians to Jordan. He served briefly in the Knesset, but in 1988 his party list was disqualified by the election commission on the grounds of racism. Kahane was assassinated by an Egyptian in New York in 1990, and four years later, after Kach activist Baruch Goldstein massacred Muslims at the Tomb of the Patriarchs, the movement was outlawed in Israel.

Demonstration, Tel Aviv, 1971. Left-wing activists protest outside the Defense Ministry after Palestinian refugees in the Gaza Strip were moved from their homes to make way for a security road.

Elections, 1969. One of the problems in Israeli politics has been the proliferation of parties. In 1969, for instance, sixteen party lists competed for the 120 Knesset seats, which are awarded on a proportional basis in elections usually held every four years. Here vote counters open envelopes and sort the ballots, each of which bears the identifying letter or letters of one party.

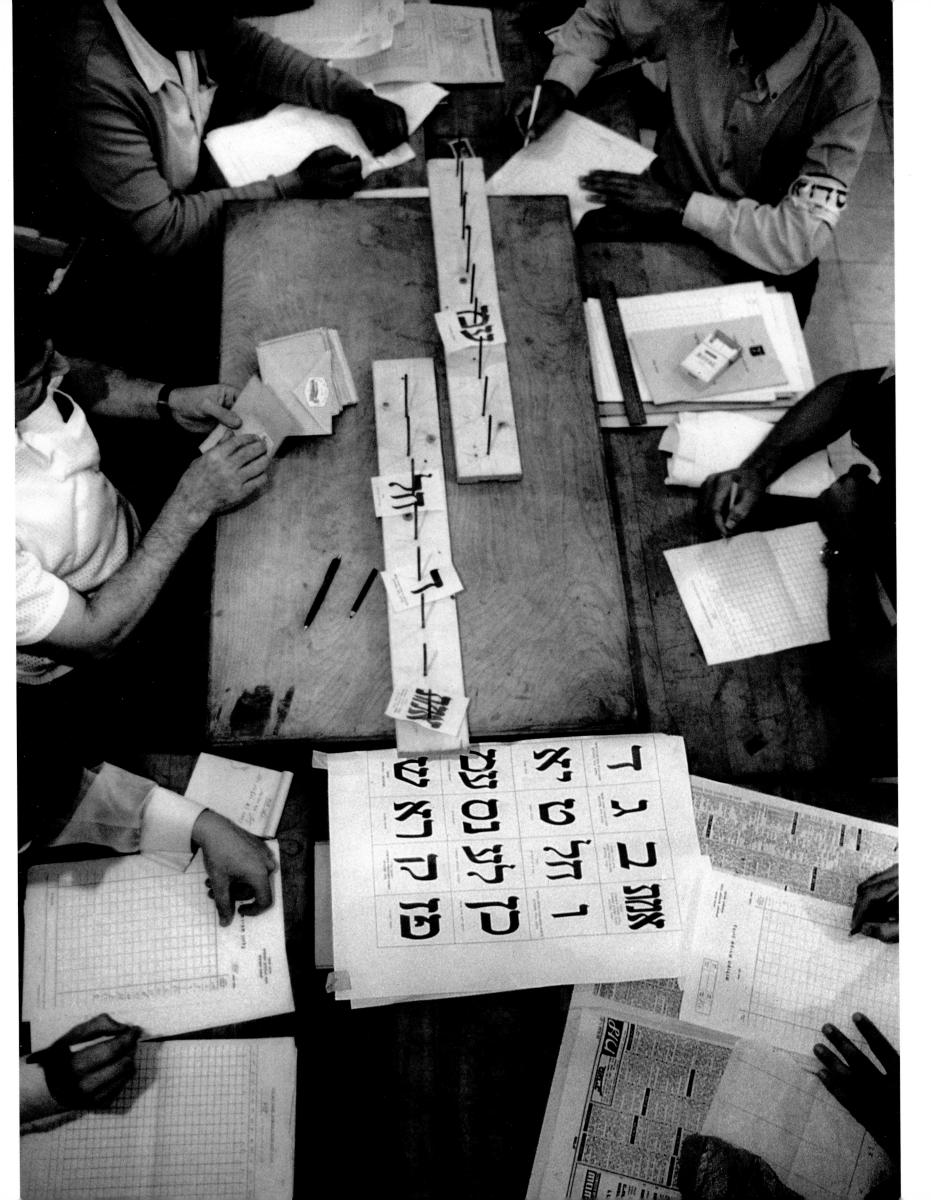

Shouting Hill, Golan Heights, 1975. On a hill near the village of Majdal Shams, members of the Druze minority gather to speak to family and friends across the border in Syria—with shouts, megaphones, handkerchiefs, and hands. The practice has continued for the last thirty years since Israel's conquest of the Golan Heights in the Six-Day War brought four Druze villages under Israeli control and cut the 16,000 residents off from their relatives.

The Druze, who live in Syria, Lebanon, and Israel, are descendants of a sect that broke away from Islam about a thousand years ago. Persecuted at first for their "heresy," they have since practiced their religion in secret.

Or Akiva, 1967. One of the "development towns" established to disperse the population of immigrants, Or Akiva languished in the 1960s. Recently its economy has flourished thanks to the influx of well-educated immigrants from the former Soviet Union.

Wedding, Peqi'in, 1966. Everyone but the bride seems to be rejoicing at this Greek Orthodox wedding. According to the Arab custom, she will be leaving her family and moving in with her husband's—a transition that can be unnerving.

Peqi'in, the village in the Galilee hills where this wedding took place, has a mixed population—mainly Druze and Christian Arabs, with a Muslim minority. There is also one Jewish family, which, according to local lore, has lived in the village since the time of the Second Temple.

***D**elivery room, Sheba Medical Center, Tel Hashomer, 1967.*

Independence Day picnic, Jerusalem, 1978.

Kibbutz Gadot, June 1967. In the midst of the Six-Day War, a reserve officer in the paratroops steals home for a few moments to play with his children. The kibbutz, established in 1949 near the border with Syria, was often targeted by Syrian positions on the Golan Heights before the war and was heavily shelled during it.

GOLDA MEIR

Meir was prime minister from 1969 to 1974, when she resigned in the wake of the Yom Kippur War.

Born in Ukraine in 1898, she moved with her family to Milwaukee as a child, then immigrated to Palestine in 1921. A member of Kibbutz Merhavia, she was active in the Labor Party, serving as Israel's first envoy to Russia and later in the Knesset.

She combined tough diplomacy with motherliness, simplicity with oversimplification. The press liked to say that she did her real work chain-smoking with her closest advisers, the "Kitchen Cabinet." She died in Tel Aviv in 1978.

Prime Minister Golda Meir and Chief of Staff Haim Bar-Lev in an air force helicopter, Sinai, 1970.

*F*orward position on the Suez Canal, October 7, 1973.

THE YOM KIPPUR WAR

When Egypt and Syria attacked on October 6, 1973, Israel was stunned. Intelligence warnings had been ignored, and this was the day of the year when the country was most vulnerable. On the Day of Atonement, the holiest in the Hebrew calendar, public life comes to a halt. Stores and offices are closed, bus and train service stops, radio and TV stations shut down. First reports of the attacks came only by word of mouth as reservists were called up from synagogues and homes.

Fighting continued on the Golan Heights, in Sinai, and west of the Suez Canal until Israeli forces repelled the attacks and a cease-fire went into effect on October 25. The military victory came at great cost, and Israelis, so confident after the Six-Day War, reeled from the shock.

Previous pages:

***E**gyptian mines, northern Sinai, October 1973.* The road leads to an Israeli stronghold code-named "Budapest." Nearby are saline swamps, the "sea of reeds" where the ancient Israelites, fleeing from Egypt, are thought to have crossed into Sinai.

"*B*udapest" stronghold during an artillery barrage, northern Sinai, October 1973. "Budapest" was the northernmost position in the Bar-Lev line, a chain of fortifications along the Suez Canal from the Mediterranean to the Red Sea, and the only one to withstand the Egyptian onslaught. Though it was besieged by commandos and heavily shelled, Israeli forces succeeded in breaking through to rescue its defenders.

Commander of the "Budapest" stronghold, northern **Sinai, October 1973.** After the war the commander of the stronghold, Lieutenant Mordechai (Motti) Ashkenazi, insisted that the government and top army officers be held accountable for Israel's lack of preparedness. What started as a one-man protest opposite the prime minister's office in Jerusalem turned into a nationwide movement that led Prime Minister Golda Meir to resign.

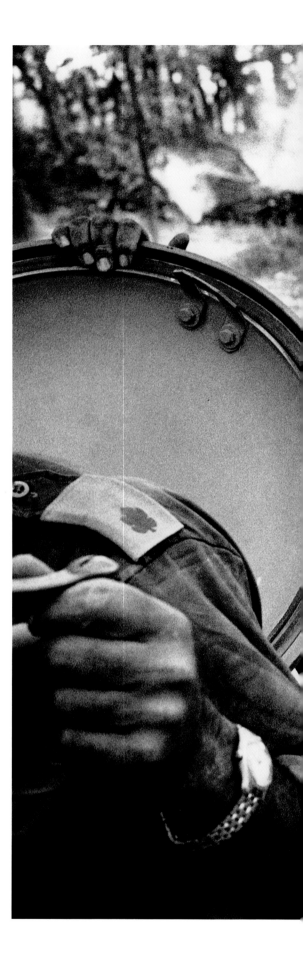

Crossing the Suez Canal, October 1973. General Ariel (Arik) Sharon (*left*) and Defense Minister Moshe Dayan cross the canal westward with Israeli forces. The crossing, after ten days of battle, was the turning point in the war.

***A**rtillery barrage, Suez Canal, October 1973.* Israeli soldiers and Egyptian
prisoners are caught together in an Egyptian attack on the bridgehead.

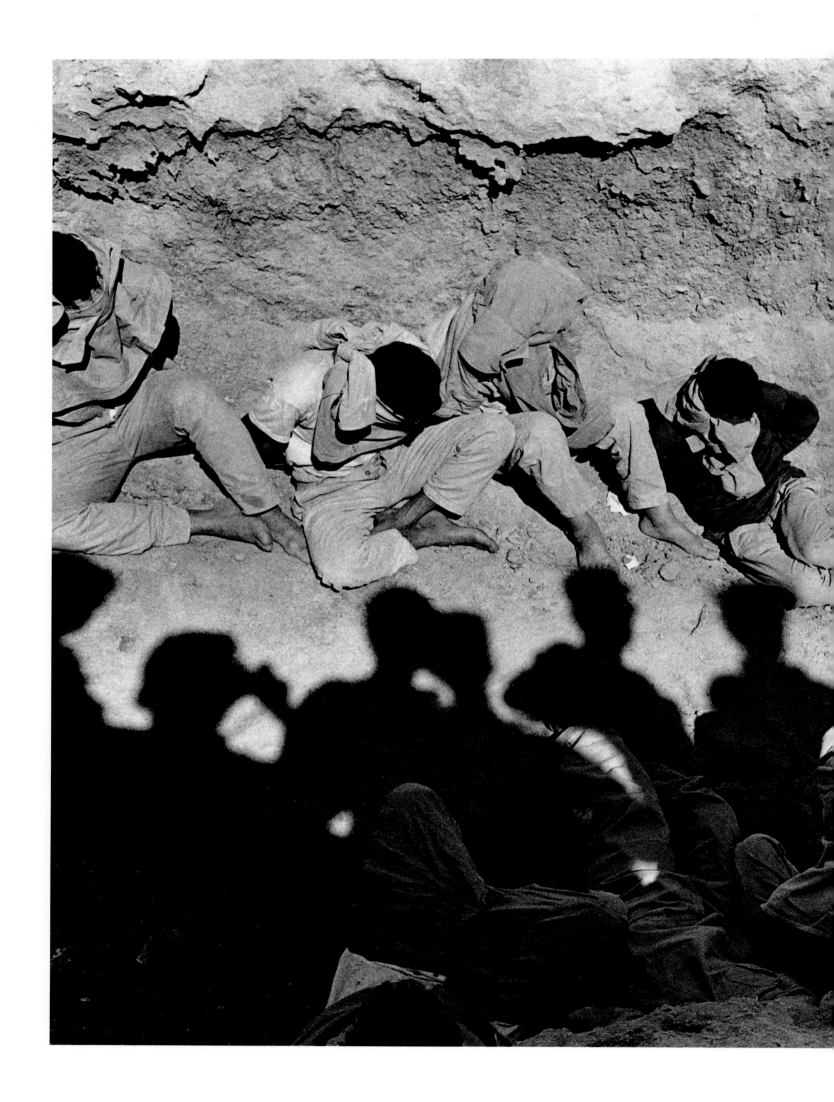

Egyptian prisoners, Suez Canal, October 1973.

Suez Canal, October 1973.

Egyptian soldiers surrender, Suez Canal, October 1973.

West of the Suez Canal, January 1974. After a long night around a campfire, Israeli forces withdrew from the Egyptian side of the canal at dawn, in accordance with the disengagement agreement.

MENACHEM BEGIN

After twenty-nine years of Labor-led governments,

Begin, longtime leader of the opposition, became

prime minister in 1977.

   Born in Lithuania in 1913, Begin came to

Palestine in 1942 and eventually led the Irgun

underground in its attempts to subvert British rule.

After the state was established, he became head of

the right-wing Herut Party (later the Likud bloc),

finally serving as prime minister from 1977 to

1983. Following the controversial Lebanon War,

with its heavy death toll, Begin abandoned

politics, remaining cloistered in his Jerusalem

home for the nine years until his death, in 1992.

Prime Minister Menachem Begin, 1977.

TALKING PEACE

Egyptian President Anwar Sadat's dramatic visit to Israel in November 1977 jolted the two countries out of their long-term belligerency. Peace negotiations, often grueling, began in Cairo a month later, and when they reached an impasse, U.S. President Jimmy Carter stepped in with assistance and pressure.

The agreement signed by Sadat and Prime Minister Menachem Begin on the White House lawn on March 26, 1979, was the first peace agreement between Israel and an Arab state.

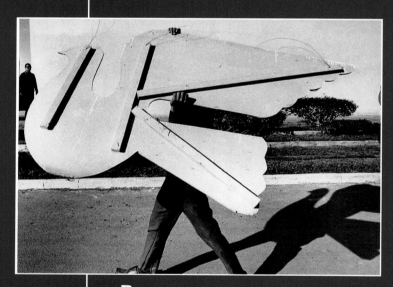

Peace dove, Isma'iliya summit, 1977.

Anwar Sadat and Menachem Begin, King David Hotel, Jerusalem, 1977.

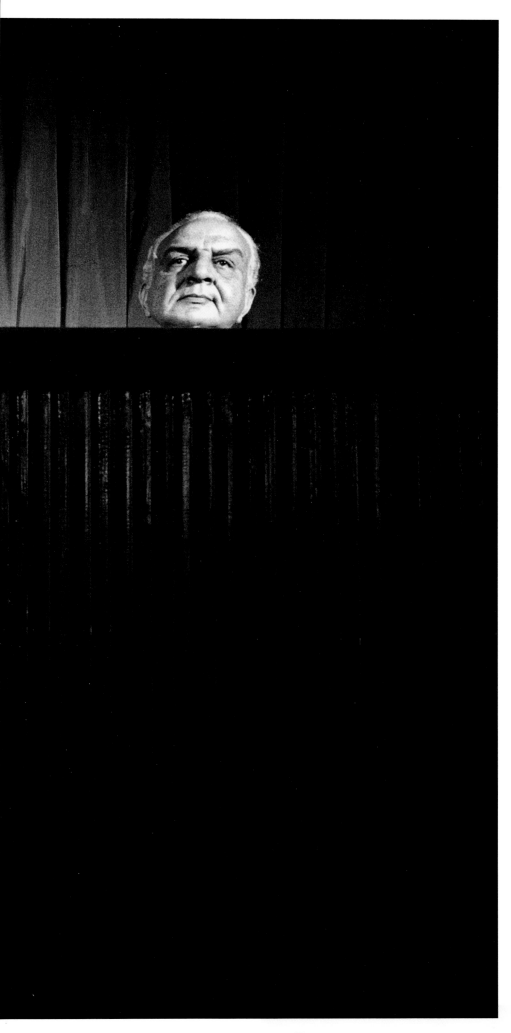

Press conference, Isma'iliya, Egypt, 1977. Isma'iliya, not far from some of the worst fighting in the 1973 war, was one of the venues for the peace negotiations. Reporting on the progress of the talks are Egyptian Vice-President Hosni Mubarak (*left*), President Sadat, and Prime Minister Mamdukh Salem.

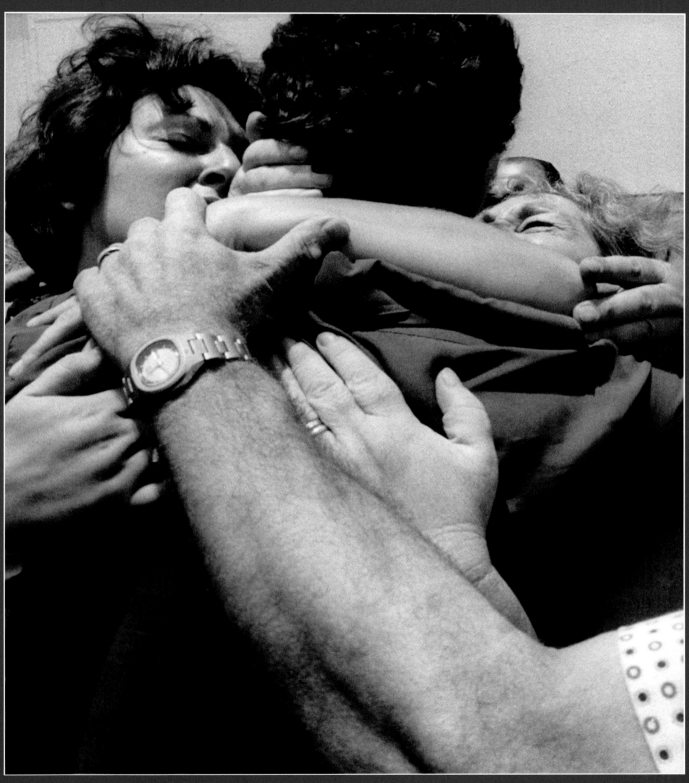

The return from Entebbe, Ben-Gurion Airport, 1976. When terrorists hijacked a Paris–Tel Aviv flight and forced it to land in Entebbe, Uganda, about 2,400 miles from its destination, Israeli commandos freed the 268 hostages in an operation that was brilliantly planned and executed. Its original code-name was "Operation Thunderbolt," but after the task-force commander, Colonel Yonatan Netanyahu, was killed (the raid's only casualty), it became known as "Operation Yonatan."

Funeral, Tiv'on, 1979. Terrorists who landed in rubber dinghies at the seaside town of Nahariya, near the Lebanese border, killed a father, his two daughters, and a policeman after taking them hostage. The mother of the family survived by hiding in an attic.

State funeral for the Munich Olympics athletes, Tel Aviv, 1972. Eleven Israeli athletes taken hostage by Palestinian terrorists during the Olympics were killed when negotiations for their release broke down.

LEAVING SINAI

For Israel, the most painful aspect of returning Sinai to the Egyptians was the final stage, evacuating the settlements in the northern sector in April 1982. Thousands of Israelis had spent more than a decade building the town of Yamit, and their lives along with it: For some, this had been the 1970s equivalent of the pioneers' efforts to drain the swamps. Now they were being told by their own government to roll up their lives and leave.

Though most settlers resigned themselves to withdrawal in the cause of peace, accepting government compensation for their property, a hard core of holdouts nearly sparked a civil war. The resisters brought in reinforcements, many of them West Bank settlers who worried that their homes would be the next to go if a peace was reached with Jordan or the Palestinians. Defense Minister Ariel Sharon called in troops to evacuate the resisters—"troops" in Israel's citizen-army likely to include the sons and daughters of friends and relatives. In the ensuing melee, resisters chained themselves together and to buildings; they threatened to blow up gas cylinders, to kill themselves and the soldiers; and they took to the rooftops, hurling down cinderblocks and burning tires. The soldiers fought back with water and foam from high-pressure fire hoses.

The last of the settlers left on April 25. Sharon had ordered all structures except the synagogue demolished, insisting that the Egyptians had demanded the destruction; the Egyptians denied it.

Entrance to Yamit, Sinai, 1982.

The evacuation of Yamit, Sinai, 1982. Resisters crowd the rooftops
and soldiers attack from below: like storming a city in ancient times.

Yamit, the last morning, 1982. At dawn on April 25, the remaining resisters gathered at the site of a war memorial that had been destroyed, its pillars strewn at right. They unfurled flags and prayed, then formed a mourning procession and slowly departed the ruined town.

Eviction from Yamit, 1982. Two soldiers, as distraught as their captive, lead a settler away.

THE LEBANON WAR

Beirut, 1982. Israeli forces move warily into West Beirut, the primarily Muslim sector, where the PLO had its stronghold.

On June 6, 1982, Israeli tanks rolled into Lebanon in an invasion officially known as "Operation Peace in Galilee." The plan was to wipe out Palestinian and other terrorist bases in the south that had been used for rocket attacks and infiltration into Israel. The bases had been strengthened when the Lebanese civil war of the mid-1970s, the latest round of Muslim-Christian fighting, left Beirut in ruins and a power vacuum throughout the country that was filled by the Syrian army.

Instead of stopping their incursion twenty-five miles north of the border as originally planned, Israeli forces continued to Beirut, battling the Syrian army along the way, to destroy the headquarters of the Palestine Liberation Organization. Israelis were deeply divided over what they saw as the first war Israel was fighting by choice rather than absolute necessity.

After vehement protests in Israel, the army pulled back in 1985 but held on to what Israel calls a "security zone" along the border, which it continues to police with the help of the South Lebanon Army, a mainly Christian militia. Syrian forces once again control the rest of Lebanon.

In their attempt to maintain a buffer zone in southern Lebanon, the Israeli army and the South Lebanon Army frequently clash with Islamic extremists such as Hezbollah, supported by Iran, and other organizations backed by Syria. Public opinion in Israel is divided on the effectiveness of this security zone whose maintenance has in fact cost many lives. A solution is likely to come only through a peace agreement with Syria.

Lebanon, 1982. A column of Israeli armored personnel carriers runs into a PLO ambush east of Sidon.

B**reakthrough into West Beirut, 1982.**

Gun position, Jewish cemetery, Damascus Road, Beirut, 1982.

Gun position, National Museum, Beirut, 1982. An Israeli soldier mans a Russian machine gun in a position recently captured from the Syrians. Both the Jewish cemetery and the museum were on the "seam" between the Muslim and Christian sectors of the city and had been appropriated by militias during the civil war.

YITZHAK RABIN AND
SHIMON PERES

Yitzhak Rabin and Shimon Peres were contrasting personalities and longtime rivals for leadership of the Labor Party. Rabin, the steely soldier, was a keen strategist. Peres, an administrator with an interest in arts and letters, has been more the diplomat.

Rabin, born in Jerusalem in 1922, was a key commander in the War of Independence and chief of staff during the Six-Day War. In 1968 he went to Washington as Israel's ambassador. Peres was born in Byelorus in 1923 and came to Palestine in 1934. A protégé of David Ben-Gurion, he promoted the defense and air industries and the development of Israel's nuclear reactor.

When Golda Meir resigned in 1974, Rabin became prime minister—the first native-born Israeli to hold that position—and appointed Peres defense minister. The two later seesawed when an electoral standoff in 1984 resulted in a national unity government with the Likud. Their cooperation made it possible for Israel to withdraw from most of Lebanon in 1985.

When Labor returned to power in 1992 with Rabin as prime minister, the two men seemed to put aside their rivalry enough to work toward an agreement with the Palestinians. However, growing opposition from the right and an atmosphere of violence culminated in Rabin's assassination in 1995. Peres succeeded him, but in 1996, he lost narrowly to the Likud's Binyamin Netanyahu.

South Lebanon, 1984. Prime Minister Shimon Peres (*left*) and Defense Minister Yitzhak Rabin return from a visit to Israeli forces. The unity government Peres headed at the time made the decision to withdraw troops.

Intifada, Gaza City, 1987. A Palestinian uprising that lasted about seven years started with a few clashes in Gaza refugee camps in December 1987 and spread through the Gaza Strip, the West Bank, and East Jerusalem. Young Palestinian protesters heaving rocks and firebombs took on Israeli soldiers firing rubber-coated bullets and live ammunition. The Palestinians, who had grown up under the occupation, felt they had nothing to lose. The Israelis, trained to fight armies, found themselves policing fourteen-year-olds in a confrontation that was dehumanizing to both sides.

Hundreds of Palestinians were killed in clashes and dozens were murdered by fellow Palestinians on suspicion of collaborating with Israel. Thousands more were wounded and tens of thousands detained without charges.

The Intifada (Arabic for "uprising") began to subside in the early nineties, particularly after the Madrid Conference of 1991 and the Oslo accords between Israel and the PLO in 1993 offered hope of Palestinian self-rule.

***D**emonstration, Umm el-Fahm, 1984.* When Rabbi Meir Kahane, leader of the racist Kach movement, announced his intention to pay a provocative visit to the Israeli-Arab town of Umm el-Fahm, residents were infuriated. Hundreds of youths set up a roadblock at the entrance to the town and, armed with sticks, rocks, and burning tires, awaited him. Police intercepted Kahane on the way and the visit never took place.

Demonstration, **Western Wall, Jerusalem, 1989.** In 1967 Jews were ecstatic at being able to visit the Wall once again. But gradually the Orthodox Jewish establishment that dominates religious practice in Israel began to regulate access to the Wall as well. The plaza in front of it has been turned into an outdoor synagogue, with men and women separated by a barrier according to Orthodox custom, and services conducted only on the men's side.

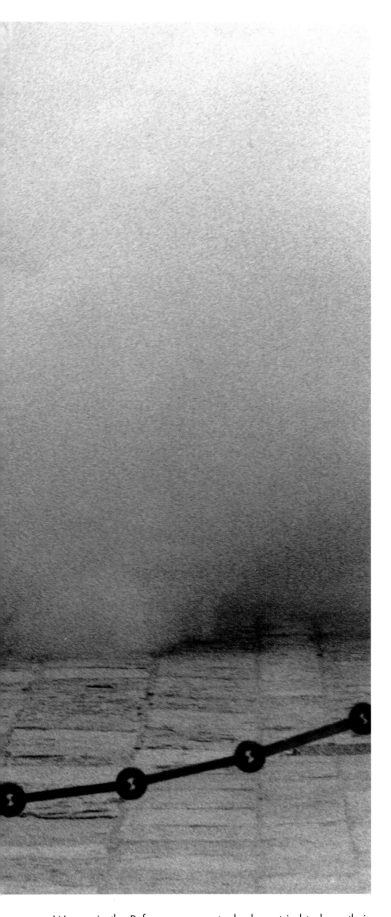

***T**omb of the Patriarchs, Hebron.* This site is considered to be the Tomb of three of the four Matriarchs (Sarah, Rebecca, and Leah) as well as the Patriarchs (Abraham, Isaac, and Jacob). Holy to both Jews and Muslims, it has been a focus of the religious and political conflict between them. In an attempt to reduce friction, Jewish and Muslim sections of the building were cordoned off. But even that proved insufficient when, in 1994, a settler named Baruch Goldstein slipped through security and opened fire on Muslims at prayer, killing more than fifty people. Since that incident, areas used by the two groups have been completely separated and each group has access at different times.

Women in the Reform movement who have tried to have their own service at the Wall have been physically attacked by Orthodox extremists. When police used smoke canisters to break up a crowd at this demonstration, some of the Orthodox protesters caught them and lobbed them back at police or at the women trying to pray.

Operation Solomon, 1991. As the civil war in Ethiopia worsened, more than 14,000 Ethiopian Jews were airlifted to Israel within thirty-six hours, a rescue mission unprecedented in its intensity. The Ethiopian Jewish community, one of the oldest outside of Israel, dates its beginning to the union of King Solomon and the Queen of Sheba.

Immigrants from the former Soviet Union, Ben-Gurion Airport, 1990. When the Soviet Union dissolved, a liberalized emigration policy brought to Israel a wave of immigrants unlike anything seen since the early years of the state. Hundreds of thousands arrived, and today Jews from the former Soviet Union, many of them academics and professionals, constitute one-tenth of the population of Israel.

ועידת ראש הממשלה לסולידריות יהודים

ONFERENCE ON JEWISH SOLIDARITY WITH

S Reich

Y Shamir

S Peres

R Maxwell

***T**he Prime Minister's Conference on Jewish Solidarity, Jerusalem, 1989.*
From left: Seymour Reich, chairman of the Conference of Presidents of Major
American Jewish Organizations; Yitzhak Shamir, prime minister of Israel; Shimon
Peres, foreign minister of Israel; and Robert Maxwell, British newspaper magnate.

Likud Party convention, Tel Aviv, 1989. From left: Binyamin Netanyahu, Dan Meridor, and Ehud Olmert. On the wall: Theodor Herzl, the Viennese journalist who is credited with the vision for a Jewish state. Update at this writing: Netanyahu is prime minister; Meridor, whom he appointed finance minister, has resigned; and Ehud Olmert is mayor of Jerusalem.

Family portrait, Ramat Gan, Gulf War, 1991. Iraq attacked Israel with Scud missiles for six weeks at the beginning of 1991—thirty-nine hits in all. Israel, for the first time ever, refrained from retaliating, bowing to pressure from the United States, which was leading an offensive against Iraq.

Because the missiles were capable of carrying chemical or biological warheads, Israelis were equipped with gas masks and instructed to seal off one room in their homes, taping plastic sheeting over windows and doors to make it as airtight as possible. Each time the siren sounded, this was the picture.

The warheads turned out to be conventional but damage was extensive, especially in the densely populated center of the country.

Vigil, Rabin Square, Tel Aviv, 1995. On November 4, 1995, at the end of a huge rally in Tel Aviv in support of the peace talks under way with the Palestinians, Prime Minister Yitzhak Rabin was shot and killed by a Jew who opposed the agreements. The assassination shocked Israelis and in the following weeks brought droves of young people to the scene to express their identification with Rabin. The site, Kings of Israel Square, was renamed in his memory.

Funeral of Yitzhak Rabin, Jerusalem, 1995. World leaders came to pay their respects when Rabin was buried at Mount Herzl, the national cemetery. President Bill Clinton concluded his eulogy with the Hebrew phrase *shalom haver,* "goodbye, friend," which turned into a motto for supporters of the peace process.

Mourning Rabin at the Knesset, Jerusalem, 1995. The grief Israelis felt on Yitzhak Rabin's death was as intense as their euphoria had been over the prospects for a new Middle East based on peace with the PLO and Jordan. When Rabin lay in state in the Knesset plaza, tens of thousands waited at the gate to honor him.

Police commander, Jenin, West Bank, 1995. Transferring power to the Palestinian Authority under the Oslo agreements has meant solving complex political and practical problems, sometimes to the satisfaction of neither Israel nor the Palestinians.

Here Major Mustafa Abu Ziad explains the maze of traffic patterns designed to minimize friction between Jewish settlers driving through Palestinian areas and Palestinians driving through areas under Israeli control.

WHICH PROMISED LAND?

Trying to envision a future, we turn to images from the recent past that will shape it. These images reflect questions inherent at Israel's birth: identity, geography, demography.

Alongside the pressing need to absorb hundreds of thousands of immigrants and maintain security are issues on which Israelis are more polarized than in the past. Can Israel survive as a democracy with a secular, open society, or is it becoming a theocracy with a growing Messianic fringe? Can the rights of an Arab minority be fulfilled in a Jewish state? How will Israel resolve the tensions between the emerging Palestinian entity and Jewish settlers building their future in the West Bank? Is land-for-peace a reasonable solution for the Golan Heights?

On these questions and others, Israelis seem to feel the way they always have, only more so. The existence of the state is taken for granted, and then a bomber in a market makes it clear that nothing is a given. Divisions deepen between the political right and left, between religious and secular Jews, between Jewish and Arab Israelis.

Theodor Herzl, the father of modern Zionism, is often held up as a paragon of determination. "If you will it," he said fifty years before the founding of the state, "it won't be just a legend." Fifty years after the founding, it remains to be seen what exactly is the will of the people, and how it can be realized.

Beehives near Mount Tabor, 1981.

Previous pages:

***W**atermelon stand, Tel Aviv, 1974.* The backdrop is a
billboard-sized movie poster made of cloth.

Shilo, West Bank, 1978. This religious settlement was established near the site of the biblical city of the same name, which became a center for worship when the Israelites, after their trek through the Sinai Desert, captured the land from the Canaanites and set up the Ark of the Covenant there. A majority of settlers in the West Bank are religious, and are motivated by the historical connection with the biblical territories of Judea in the southern sector and Samaria in the north.

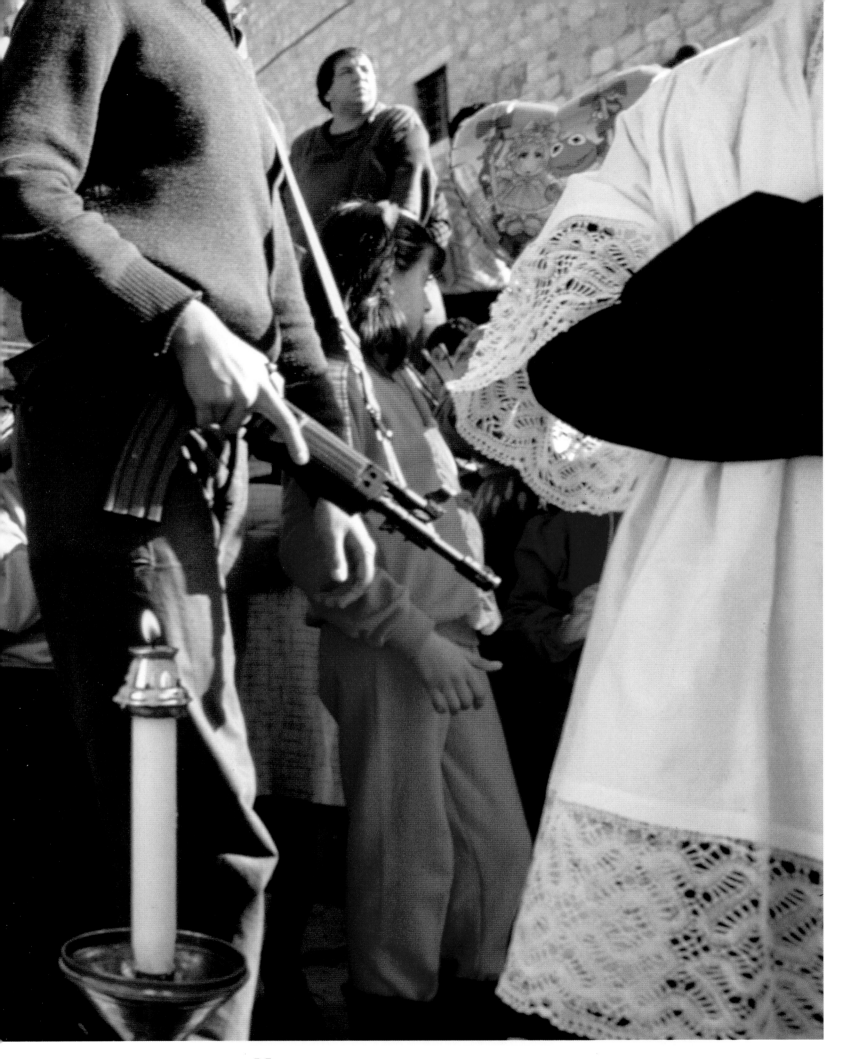

Manger Square, Bethlehem, 1988. Pilgrims, clergy, local residents, and Israeli soldiers were all on hand at Christmas. The mix changed somewhat in 1996, when the West Bank town was turned over to the Palestinian Authority, in accordance with the Oslo agreements, and Israeli troops pulled out.

Preparations for Independence Day, Ofra, 1979. Ofra, founded in 1975, is a religious community—hence the crocheted skullcaps along with the flags, underwear, and socks on a laundry day in May.

Following pages:

Lookout point, Golan Heights, 1967. After the Six-Day War, thousands of Israelis rushed to the Golan Heights to take a look at the Sea of Galilee, the Jordan Valley, and the Galilee hills from the vantage point of a Syrian stronghold. The Heights afford not only military advantage but also control of Israel's major water sources.

Today, 16,000 Israelis live in thirty-two settlements on the Golan Heights. The country is about evenly divided on the question of a withdrawal in return for peace, and the decisive moment is likely to be a national referendum.

IN APPRECIATION

Forty years ago a young woman starting out as an artist asked me to photograph one of her sculptures. Proud of the print I'd produced, I waited for the compliments. What I got was devastating criticism. "Your photo's not bad," she said, "but it doesn't look much like my sculpture." Since then Orna and I have been living and working together. We've learned to listen to each other, to argue, to fight, and to delight in our collaboration.

This book has been one of our joint efforts. Every book is a long journey, but the road seems endless when the subject is controversial and anyone within shouting distance knows better than the authors how the book should be done. It has been a tense time, and our sons Barak and Nimrod suffered the most. We apologize and thank them for their patience and penetrating comments, as we thank our oldest son, Ahuvia, who shared our visions and revisions from afar. And my mother, Hanna Anguli, has been a source of hope and optimism in the most difficult moments.

Special thanks also go to Yoav Te'eni, my friend from 1948, who fostered my romance with his Leica and guided my first steps in photography.

In addition I thank the many writers and editors I have worked with over the years, who (usually) took my crazes and caprices in stride. I'm particularly grateful to the *New York Times* colleagues with whom I worked as photographer for the Jerusalem bureau over a span of twenty-two years: Jim Feron, Terry Smith, the late Bill Farrell, David Shipler, Tom Friedman, and Joel Brinkley. Our collaborations resulted in many of the photographs in this book. (Our special appreciation goes to Tom Friedman; his essay moved Orna and me despite our attempts to keep a cool distance.) In New York, *Times* editors Abe Rosenthal, Arthur Gelb, and Mike Levitas went beyond formal work relations to give me a sense of belonging.

My colleague Shlomo Arad has shared more than a few tight spots with me and, despite professional competition, has remained a friend. Among the colleagues at Magnum who encouraged me and gave me necessary criticism were Hiroji Kubota, Elliot Erwitt, Erich Hartman, and René Burri; Jimmy Fox and Chris Boot have also been of tremendous assistance.

Marc Scheps, friend and former director of the Tel Aviv Museum of Art and the Ludwig Museum in Cologne, has had faith in me, inspired me, and broadened my cultural outlook over many years.

We would also like to express our gratitude to Dr. Michael Levin, man of arts and letters, who helped with his good taste and balanced judgment; to Dr. Nira Feldman, friend and historian, who brought us back to reality from time to time and restored our sense of proportion; to Ze'ev Schiff, military correspondent for the newspaper *Ha'aretz*, who helped us define military terms and events; to Deborah Harris and Beth Elon of the Harris/Elon Agency, for their enthusiasm and support; to Marsha Pomerantz, who translated and enriched our texts, contributing intelligence, deliberation, meticulous attention, and subtlety of language, and who helped us past obstacles and mines on the long road; to Constance Herndon, senior editor at Simon & Schuster, who took great trouble and care with our work and firmly required us to clarify certain points for the American audience; and to Yossi Jibri, master designer, who has been with us through the many stages of conception and construction of a complex book.

Production and publication of this book were made possible by the generous help and friendship of the Schussheim Foundation in Haifa. Its representatives Dorothy Schussheim and Amos Dolav have supported us warmly since the project began, and without their help the book could never have appeared in its current format. Hanno D. Mott, New Yorker and longtime friend, also gave us the assistance necessary to achieve the level of quality we were striving for. Howard Squadron has been a boundless source of friendship and wisdom.

Above all, our thanks go to Cornell Capa for his fatherly warmth and friendship. He has never spared me his criticism, but with his wife, Edith, has supported, encouraged, and assisted us, and received us with love.

Orna joins me in gratitude and good wishes to all who helped.

Micha Bar-Am   Orna Bar-Am

INDEX

Annual kite festival, Jerusalem, 1996.